GW00507965

ALL TOO TRUE

Fleur Cowles

Also by Fleur Cowles
Friends and Memories
The Case of Salvador Dali
Bloody Precedent
Tiger Flower

Fleur Cowles has contributed to
Treasures of the British Museum
I Can Tell It Now

A DEBT REPAID

Painting by Camille Bombois

ALL TOO TRUE

Twenty-nine true stories that might have been invented

Fleur Cowles

QUARTET BOOKS
LONDON MELBOURNE NEW YORK

First published by Quartet Books Limited, 1982
A member of the Namara Group
27/29 Goodge Street, London W1P 1FD

Copyright © 1982 by Fleur Cowles, Creative Industries,
Bermuda

Typeset by MC Typeset, Rochester, Kent
Printed and bound in Great Britain by
Mackays of Chatham, Kent

British Library Cataloguing in Publication Data

All too true.
I. Cowles, Fleur
081   PS3553.0/

ISBN 0-7043-2327-3

To Tom

CONTENTS

LIST OF

ILLUSTRATIONS

The new face of Jacqueline Auriol, one of the world's greatest pilots

Carl Wiseman, the 'bird man' of Denmark, who made dogs sing

Evgeni Yost, the subject of a story told by Lord Inverchapel, former United Kingdom Ambassador to the USSR

INTRODUCTION

These stories are true. They happened. They touched people's lives, sometimes traumatically, sometimes hilariously, sometimes hauntingly.

I haven't set out to collect them. They just came my way and I've selected a diverse group from a large bag. They originated in many ways: some were inherited from other story-tellers, some I witnessed, a few happened to me. All have passed the tests of audiences and time, since telling stories has always been my own passion. In some cases, I've disguised person and identification when I thought it proper.

Some may merit being turned into fiction or even into films. I envy those who can write fiction but I am by nature and profession a gatherer of facts and thus have never attempted to write except as a reporter.

A few of the stories follow the example of two literary gentlemen who brought to perfection the techniques of giving a story an *unexpected* ending (which today we call a twist-in-the-tail ending). Both men lived in the last century – O. Henry in the United States and Guy de Maupassant in France. Both men observed human events with a sharp eye and fitted them with the precision of a camera into the stories they invented. There was always the surprise ending – sometimes ridiculous, sometimes harrowing, even Tolstoyan – to their tales.

This collection is assorted in length as well as subject – adding up to a small and I hope enjoyable book to read from time to time or from cover to cover. I can see it by bedsides and in pockets on trains and planes.

My favourite story is the first in the book, 'Twin Sets'. No names are used but it will be immediately recognizable to other friends of the husband and wife team (famous in the musical world of Paris) to whom they must also have told it. It concerns an elderly lady who lived in a huge, dark Victorian mansion in the countryside a hundred miles north of Paris. No one knew her or her name – or the mysterious secret of her life. A hush of disbelief always follows its exposure.

Perhaps the most moving story is 'Soul for Sale', about a very poor Frenchman who actually sold his soul to the village's most hated second-hand dealer and who suffered a cruel sort of living death as a result – quite like a Kafka protest against reality. The American painter Enrico Donati told it to me thirty years ago and its drama has lived in my mind ever since.

There is a similar sort of horror in the short story 'A Night in a Gambler's Life', covering twelve hours in the life of a compulsive gambler and his battered wife – which she'll never forget. A nightmare tale.

Some stories are hard to believe, like 'The Pearl Necklace', about a string of pearls which has a preposterous, even macabre twist.

Ludwig Bemelman, the writer, left all his friends masses of personal tales before he died, each one enhanced by his own delight in telling them. I've written of two; one a tiny vignette of an incident on the road outside Paris, the other about a waiter who unintentionally altered the life of one of his favourite diners.

An American aviator was once dubbed 'Wrong Way Corrigan' because he flew his plane in the wrong direction in a memorable feat of aviation. My story, 'A Woman in a Taxi', is of the gentle elderly wife of an American hero who took a wrong-way taxi journey during the Coronation ceremony when Elizabeth II became Queen.

Revolutions are plotted under diverse circumstances. 'Basement Story' describes how (although not as a participant) I was inadvertently an encouragement to those who plotted against the Perons.

Writing my book about the Surrealist painter, *The Case of Salvador Dali*, involved elements of hilarity and disgust – and even adventure – as in a ridiculous visit to his home in Port Lligat in Spain.

I have included another favourite, 'Stalin's Gift', the story of the dictator's gift of a Russian man to a diplomat, handed over to him as though he was no more than a sack of potatoes. Hard to believe? Yes, even I began to doubt it (after years of hearing it told) until I had the account read, vetted and okayed by the widow of the diplomat involved, and then reconfirmed by two other British diplomats.

Preceding it is an account, quite out of an '007' film, of experiences when Wendell Willkie and companions on their 'One World' trip during the Second World War left the guest house at Kuibyshev for the guest house of the Kremlin in Moscow.

For obvious reasons, I've decided not to enlarge on the details of an hallucinatory Iron Curtain story about an ingenuous American politician who asked, while in Russia after the War, if he could speak to a group of 'ordinary Russian people' to say how deeply interested America was in their welfare. The crowd of silent men, gathered below him as he stood on a dais in the fields outside Moscow, never understood a word he said, but it didn't matter. Each was a cowed inmate of a concentration camp, forced by jailers to become his audience and commanded to applaud.

Recently, I added another war story to my collection; this was told me by a Lebanese friend. It supposedly occurred during the terrible off-again, on-again war raging in Beirut.

INTRODUCTION

Each time the guns were silenced for temporary truces, the city stopped to count its dead, its wounded, its homeless, its orphans – and the pillaging. Bombing blew humans, homes and furniture to bits (many of the possessions were simply stolen). Such loot often found its way to the markets of neighbouring Damascus, where many of the luckier Lebanese had fled.

One refugee from Beirut who had lost her money and possessions in the bombing also found her way to Damascus, expecting to live a life of poverty. Soon after she arrived she looked up a good friend who had escaped with all her possessions and was reputed to be living opulently – from whom she hoped for a friendly hand. When she entered the drawing room, she nearly fainted. There she saw her own elegant damask sofa (which she thought had been lost in a Beirut blitz) in a place of honour in the salon.

'That's my sofa! Where did you get it? It's mine, it's mine!' she cried out in distress.

'Don't talk such nonsense,' the woman replied. 'It was delivered to me last week by the man who made it for me here. It is a perfectly new piece of furniture and can't possibly be yours. How can you accuse me of such a thing?' the hostess demanded in a mixture of embarrassment and rage.

The distraught refugee rushed away to seek a lawyer. The next day, her courage propped up by his companionship, she returned and demanded to see the sofa again.

'She has a legal right to do so,' the lawyer calmly announced. They were coolly ushered into the large room. Facing the new owner with iciness (and without the slightest warning), the woman hastily stepped behind the sofa, produced a large pair of scissors from her handbag and, before she could be stopped, slashed through the fabric lining at the back of the couch. A large brown bundle fell to the floor with a bang – it was the one she had carefully sewn inside the fabric in the framework of the elegant piece of furniture barely six months before – a bundle of jewels and money (lots of it) which she'd hidden inside its carcass in a last–ditch effort to hide her remaining valuables from looters in Beirut.

'Now you are quite welcome to my couch,' she announced to the shocked owner as she stormed out with the lawyer, her bundle in her bag.

Good stories need not be tragic; some of the best are the funniest, which certainly was true of those told me by the very special Gina Bachauer – who was one of the world's great story-tellers as well as pianists. Her stories *happened* to her and she told them in her inimitable fractured English. Everyone who knew her (and that means a global circle) before her recent death will miss her, her tales and her music.

She returned to London from every tour with a bagful of stories about the agonizing comedy situations she had just encountered. No trip occurred without them. Why never to other musicians – only to her, we used to ask? Her first port-of-call every time she reached England was our house in Sussex for the traditional weekend which we awaited with impatience.

A serious concert isn't the place to expect nonsense but tragi-comedy always waited in the wings for Mme Bachauer's arrival, whether at Carnegie Hall, in Tel Aviv, in the Middle West or in an army camp, where so often she donated her talent. Such as: the night when the men forgot to fix the piano in position on a New York City concert stage. At the first touch of her strong hands the piano started moving away from her – slowly, slowly, slowly – until it was too far away for her to keep moving her bench to it. Television cameras were trained on her, and the audience bent over with affectionate laughter.

Then there was the time a grand piano arrived on stage in a Middle East city; one very large cockroach sat on a vantage point in the dead centre of the piano, just above the keyboard. Antennae twitching, it chose to remain and stare straight at her, unmoving – until she sharply broke off playing and stalked off the stage, announcing loudly as she left, 'Dot is too much. Dot beast must go – or I go!'

Or when she rode into the African desert to play for wounded soldiers at an army base hospital. The piano (older than she) had been filched out of nowhere and was totally unusable. She sat down to face the grim fact of an empty keyboard: most of the black and white keys (from which the glue had dried and come away from the piano) were piled in neat stacks on each side.

A good time to bow out? No, she couldn't disappoint those terribly wounded men whose beds had been wheeled into a hall for the rare visit of an entertainer. Yet, to play on a roughly surfaced, uncovered keyboard would have torn her fingertips to bits, preventing her from fulfilling concert commitments for a long time to come.

'Anyvon have chewing gum here?' she suddenly demanded. Gum was, in fact, located. 'Now, please, chew, chew!' she commanded the men. Furnished with the results from countless hurriedly chewed packets, she managed to stick each individual key down with a wad of gum – and began to play, accompanied by cheers. The applause turned to raucous laughter as, one by one, the keys flew into the air at her dramatic attack. The concert, meant to take one hour, actually required several. Keys constantly flew off and more and more gum had to be chewed to put them back into place.

There was the time a man nagged her relentlessly to listen to the magic of his tiny son playing the piano. When she finally found the necessary time, the prodigy was 'ill' and his father came alone, bringing a record to play for her instead. In shocked disbelief, she heard an extraordinary performance.

'But dot is not possible. Dot is music from a master!'

The father beamed with joy. 'Yes – yes. It is a record by Horowitz – but my son plays exactly like that!'

Once for a charity concert, a Middle Western conductor in the United States cabled her in England to bring over the music of a particular favourite concerto of hers. Forgetting the cable, he had relentlessly rehearsed his own orchestra in a totally different one – which, of course, it was too late for her to have any choice but to play.

I often persuaded her to tell her stories to my guests, once after a concert in my home to the greatly amused Queen Elizabeth the Queen Mother. On another evening, the guests included a few well-known funny men for whom her stories were like manna from heaven.

It was a night of endless laughter, ending at two o'clock in the morning after many guests had been 'on stage' to tell their own stories. The then future King Constantine of Greece described how he and a princely cousin were arrested for speeding on empty streets after a very late party in Philadelphia. Being royal, they carried no identification, no licence and certainly no money. The antics they went through before convincing very dubious policemen that they *were* who they said they were were very, very funny indeed.

Jack Benny, in his usual laconic style, had given us joke after joke, just before Gina Bachauer began to tell hers. Later, as he was leaving, he turned back to me, sadly: 'I go on paying fabulous sums of money to my funny men to provide me with gags. And, here, without paying a cent, Gina Bachauer is the

INTRODUCTION

funniest person I've ever heard.

'Do you know why? Because her stories are true – and *true* stories are the best,' he concluded.

Fleur Cowles
London
December 1981

TWIN

Everyone knew something of their well-to-do neighbours in the heavily-wooded, tiny forest somewhere north of Paris where five houses stood. They ranged from a miniature château to a large, lonely Victorian mansion. The area was not large, but an air of isolation was intensified by the thickly-wooded copse to the back and encroaching on the sides of each house.

Trees protected and drew lines of privacy but they also kept neighbour from neighbour, allowing a world of his own to each occupant. The curious little group living there was bent on keeping its privacy. If interest in the persons next door (who lived there, how life was spent) did exist, lethargy prevented any communication.

Perhaps the only bond between them was a common longing to know something about the elderly lady who hid herself inside the ugly, vast, untended Victorian house. The shutters were always shut; this house, alone among the five, was drifting toward dereliction. It had a secret life vested in mystery.

There was speculation; some details were known: an elderly lady lived inside, there was a vast population of dogs – a glorious assortment of mongrels – which wandered freely within the estate, plainly held inside by unlimited affection and pampering.

Within her twenty-odd acres, the old lady managed to hide so well that her neighbours (who might otherwise have given her the cold shoulder they gave each other) kept their intense curiosity alive.

SETS

No one had ever met her. No one had ever seen her in the village – never in the shops, on the street, or walking a dog. An old uncommunicative retainer chose her food and ordered it by telephone. Shopkeepers collaborated in silence, knowing little or nothing themselves. It was 'said' she had plenty of money, that she demanded to be left alone and had lived as a recluse for the last twenty years.

Two very great friends of mine, part of the entertainment world of Paris, lived in the house right next door. Their long driveway was parallel to hers, separated by a twelve-foot high wall of hedge, with both driveways hugging the hedge and ending in gates that were shoulder to shoulder.

My friend, Monsieur G., never drove down the gravel driveway without the constant hope that he'd find the old lady at the end of the road. 'Just one look at her would be wonderful,' he'd muse.

One day, she was there: the fact that she waited for him at the gate was so startling, it simply didn't register.

'Stop! Stop! You must help me!' she cried out to him as he nearly passed her by.

He braked to a stop, astonished and delighted, mentally rubbing his hands together.

'But of course, madam. What can I do to help you?'

'Eleven of my dogs have disappeared! You must help me find them. You must go on television in Paris and announce to everyone living this side of Paris that they must look for them. Please, please,' she begged.

It was more a command than a plea. The old lady, in tears,

had at long last materialized. Her age? A very old sixty-five, or was she a young seventy-five? It was hard for him to judge the harassed, tearful face. Her figure was non-existent – lean but shapeless. Her face? The features were certainly very elegant. Grey hair was piled on top of her head, loosely, without thought. Her dress was just a black covering.

'When did they disappear?' my friend asked. 'Give me a description of all of them.'

'They simply raced out after another pack of dogs – about six o'clock this morning. They've never been away for three hours before. Something terrible must have happened,' the weeping old lady explained.

Armed with minute descriptions of the size, shape, colour and personality of every dog, Monsieur G. drove to the nearest police station and reported their disappearance.

'For heaven's sake, mention my name with every dog you return to their mistress,' he pleaded with the police. 'I want her to know *I'm* responsible. . .'

The drama died like a burnt-out candle that same morning. Wherever the group had wandered off to and for whatever reason, the call of food was stronger. At mid-morning, eleven panting, over-affectionate, impatiently-hungry dogs came home and were received like lost sailors.

The biggest disappointment befell Monsieur G. when he drove home, earlier than usual, from Paris to contact his neighbour. The gates to her driveway were locked. No one awaited him – and no one was there the next morning. No thanks, no explanations. Communication had come to an end. His dream of friendship begun in tears was over. Worst of all, he hadn't even reached the front door of the mysterious house.

He and his wife soon developed a new anxiety: they had to know what went on inside the front door. It was even more irritating to have come so close but to be farther away than ever.

The game unexpectedly reached its next stage a month later. Coming home one light summer evening, Monsieur G. again found his neighbour at his gates. There was the same drab beauty and the same careless coiffure but this time no tears. With great timidity and shyness, she explained: 'I do owe you my thanks. You were so helpful when I was in trouble last month. Won't you come in and let me give you a cup of tea?'

'But how kind of you. I'd be delighted,' he quickly responded. 'Won't you allow me to drive you to your door?'

'No, I'd rather walk. I'll meet you inside. You are expected.'

He simply couldn't believe his luck. He drove into her drive, parked his car before the door he and his wife had so often discussed. He found the door being opened.

Another very old lady, wordless but neat and correct in parlour-maid's uniform, stood there and showed him in. Once inside, she opened the door to a sitting room on the left of the vast, dark hall. When he'd chosen a chair, the door silently closed and he was left alone.

In the few minutes left before the hostess arrived on foot, he tried to digest his thoughts. First of all, his luck: he'd actually been invited inside! He made a quick survey of the room he was in: the beautiful, barely worn French furnishings were so incongruous inside the chaotic Victorian architecture. Then the final shock!

What he saw on the walls was real, he wasn't dreaming, although he couldn't believe his eyes: he was sitting in a strange sort of art museum, surrounded by the world's most unique collection of paintings. Too incredible to describe, and certainly unbelievable. . .

Every painting on the walls (and the walls were literally 'papered' in paintings) hung in a pair. An identical copy of each painting hung side-by-side with the original. *Which was which?*

One thing was crystal clear; he must not make any reference to them. When the woman arrived, he composed himself, his eyes and mind disciplined not to wander around the room. As calmly as possible, he obeyed his instinct and kept the conversation strictly to the episode of the lost-and-found dogs, her love of the animals and his pleasure in trying to help her in a moment of need. After a reasonable half-hour of tea and small-talk, he bowed out.

Not once had he betrayed his astonishment. Not once did his glance leave hers. He never looked around him again. When he turned at the front door of the house for a final thank you, he saw the mirage again – *twin sets of paintings everywhere, (the largest of all lining the high stair wall)*. From Goyas to Gainsboroughs, masterpieces of their period.

All the way home, down one drive and up his own, his mind wavered in nervous indecision. Would anyone believe him? Would he ever be asked back? Would he ever have a chance to ask her the Big Question? Wouldn't it have been better just to have made some modest comment about her collection?

No, he was sure he'd done the right thing. 'No matter what my wife says, I know I'm right,' he reasoned. The old lady's confidence in me will build up. One day we'll be friendly enough for me to broach the question.

To his astonishment his wife agreed, 'Play it slowly. Become her friend. You'll soon find *her* anxious to talk after all these years of silence and loneliness.'

They were right. Not in any onrush of neighbourliness, but once every few months, the old woman would see Monsieur G. at the gate. She seemed to sense when he'd be coming from his Paris office. She began by the occasional nod and a few words more, and finally after some months she asked him in for his second cup of tea. This time, in nervous excitement, he knew he would not be able to contain himself.

Once again, she declined the lift in his car. He was welcomed into the house by the same old retainer to await the owner's slow walk up the path. This time, he was shown into the second drawing room, opening on the opposite side of the hall. Once again, he was in a room full of beautiful French furniture entirely out of character with its Victorian walls. Twin sets of paintings (mainly Impressionists, and each set lovelier than the next) hung all around him.

The door opened. Tea wagon and maid followed the hostess. Tea was quickly served. The old lady got right to the point in a flash.

'I know you must be longing to know the story of my paintings. I will tell you, as I too am longing desperately to discuss them with someone. You must realize I trust you,' she reminded him as she started off in a gush of words. Not once did he interrupt her.

'Forty-five years ago, I became the mistress of "Monsieur X". He was, as you know, one of France's greatest connoisseurs and collectors of art.

24

SETS

'I believe he loved me very dearly, but he was also deeply attached to his wife. He gave her a most beautiful house, (one she made quite famous, the Hotel de . . .). But he also arranged a home for me of beauty and elegance – as much to satisfy his own eye (since he spent a great deal of time with me) as to make me happy with the treasured gifts. This need always to be surrounded by the beautiful things he loved led to an incredible mania.

'Every time he bought a piece of furniture or china or any little treasure, he tried to find two which were nearly identical. One went to his wife, the other to me – which was easy for a man of his great wealth. The dealers knew he liked to buy in pairs (of at least similar value and period).

'The complication naturally arose when it came to collecting paintings. He couldn't cope except in one way; he actually developed a source – or sources – to have each painting he bought meticulously copied! As hard as I tried I couldn't persuade him to divulge the arrangement. I never did find out how this was done – by whom or at what cost – but as you can see – these are remarkable hoaxes! The originals and their copies were always fantastically matched.

'His wife died suddenly and we were at last able to marry. After this glorious occasion we naturally decided to close one home and to pool the treasures of both establishments; but we postponed the difficult task until after our honeymoon.

'We chose a small château in south-west France, a place where we'd stopped before on motor trips. It was isolated, beautiful, comfortable and full of pleasant memories.

'One night he left me to take his usual walk in the country lane. I chose to wait for him because I hated the darkness of the road – and that premonition was hideously accurate. A car came along at a fast pace and didn't catch him in the beam of its headlights until it was too late to swerve. My husband was instantly killed.

'When I could pull myself out of the collapse I fell into (and it was months before I could even think for myself), I decided life in Paris was impossible – I never wanted to go near a place we'd shared together.

'I found this old house out of town. I bought it because it was vast enough to give a home to all his favourites out of the former two households. The rest I sold.

'Every painting came with me. I hung them side-by-side. Only I know which one he gave to *her*, which he gave to *me*.

'I shall never let anyone in to see them again. I don't ever want them examined or discussed. I simply could not bear to find out which one of each pair is *real*.'

My husband had a great friend who used to tell this tale of his old father. He was a splendid gentleman in every way but a crashing bore on the subject of wines. Because he was truly a great expert whose speciality was port, he could invariably, by smell or taste, tell both the shipper and the age of each bottle to within four to six years.

A rather regal old friend of his, who had fought beside him in the First World War, used to invite him once or twice each year to his lovely estate in the country. A Rabelaisian character himself, he also had a love of wine and a great sense of humour.

His house was already full of guests the night before the elderly wine expert was expected. At breakfast on the Saturday, the host announced that his last guest would be arriving before lunch, explained who he'd be – and that he had decided to pull the man's leg as well as to win a wager for himself and other guests. The men in the house party wanted to know how.

He would go down to the village that morning to post some letters and while there would buy a bottle of ordinary unlabelled grocer's port. It would then be decanted and served after dinner from the usual handsome crystal bottle. The plan was for the assembled male guests each to place

EXPERT

five pound bets to hear the expert tell both its vintage and its shipper.

The stage was set. Dinner over, the women rose from the table to leave the men to their port and talk. The port arrived and was presented first to the wine expert for his usual pronouncement. He tasted it, then smelled it and smiled affably.

'There's no doubt it is Cockburn,' he announced without wasting time. 'Old? Perhaps '28, perhaps '30.'

Both comments were greeted with guffaws and roars of laughter. The bell was rung and the host commanded the butler to 'remove the rubbish' and to bring in a decanter of 'real port'. The bets were paid promptly and gracefully by the old man, paying out his five pound notes with a wry smile.

Putting aside his experience, he quickly joined in the fun and casually helped to consume the contents of the new decanter of fine port. When it was time to join the ladies he arranged inconspicuously to be the last to leave the dining room. Upon reaching the door, he turned in the great style and elegance so typical of an old English gentleman to speak to the butler who was standing at attention.

'James, here is five pounds but please do not sell any more of your master's port to the grocer.'

CLOAK-AND-DAGGER

In the United States, just after the War, when I was still married to Gardner ('Mike') Cowles, a notable raconteur, I used to listen often as he told innumerable stories about Wendell Willkie, the defeated Republican who ran against President Franklin D. Roosevelt in 1944. Cowles, as his friend, had so vigorously supported him that Willkie selected him to go with him on his famous 'One World' flight around the globe in the early years after the War. A potential bookful of stories have come out of that journey.

The trip came about in an unusual way: after losing the election, Willkie didn't waste time licking his wounds. Instead, he made an unexpected wartime decision to fly around the world and to report his findings to the nation – thus retaining his undeniable position as the most significant Republican figure in the land.

Because we were at war, permission to take the journey depended on the nod of the Commander-in-Chief of the United States Forces – and that man was the President himself. The astute Franklin D. Roosevelt realized how much political capital Willkie would make of such a journey but he also knew that, if he withheld his approval, it would be interpreted as political cowardice.

He knew how to cope: he made the trip appear as if it was as much his idea as Willkie's by the remarkable ploy of announcing that he was, in fact, sending his political adversary as his personal emissary to Stalin.

Nothing but kudos greeted Willkie on his return. Few

IN RUSSIA

political figures have made a more dramatic impact on the public by one journey, nor made more political history. The book, which he wrote immediately afterwards, *One World*, became one of the most distinguished political essays of its time. It described to a war-oriented public the united world Willkie deeply hoped would materialize after the fighting was over – an irony today; but the idea of uniting the world after the War lit up the minds and hearts of many enlightened thinkers (and gave a boost to the sorely-tried liberal flank of the Republican Party).

One of the many stories of their trip constantly flashes into view – probably because it is a visual one I can evoke easily in my mind's eye. It concerns the James Bond cloak-and-dagger detour which marked their arrival on Russian soil.

Flying into Russian territory, they were turned back on the first lap of their journey to Moscow by Stalin's command. They were shunted to Kuibyshev in Siberia for their own safety and there they had to wait impatiently for five days until the Germans' threat to lay siege to Moscow (as they had so horrifyingly done to Leningrad) was overcome.

Everyone in the party became tired and anxious awaiting the sigal to proceed. When the word came through, Willkie's crew rushed off to rev up the engines for immediate departure. All was ready when Willkie reached the airport. Incidentally and significantly, they were flying in a plane which was the fastest known in that day, arranged by

Roosevelt to ensure their safe return.

Before Willkie left the government's Guest House, he followed his usual farewell routine with the staff. All were invited to line up on the doorstep of the front entrance so that they could be thanked personally by him: the chef, the maids, the valets. Each got a warm parting handshake, all of it face-to-face. Each had come to know the other very well after having been incarcerated for five days.

As soon as this ceremony was over, they stepped into the regulation black cars supplied and were sped to the airport, driving at the usual wild clip reserved for Russian officials. At the airport, a Guard of Honour stood by to be very quickly reviewed, American and Russian national anthems were played (the Star-Spangled Banner never sounded the same to any of them again), warm handshakes were exchanged with the official host, in this case Mr Vishinsky, and then the men dashed into their plane, which took off instantly.

Exactly the same fast procedure was repeated on arrival in Moscow. This time, greeted by Foreign Minister Molotov, they once again stood at attention while national anthems were played and Willkie reviewed the Guard of Honour. They were then taken ('180 miles an hour, careering in large cars through Moscow streets,' recalled Mike Cowles) to the Guest House of the Kremlin.

To the utter astonishment of every single person in the party, they found, waiting on the doorstep the identical staff they had left behind in Kuibyshev; wreathed in smiles of welcome. How could they possibly have arrived there *before* Willkie?

No one will ever know.

Another of Mike Cowles's stories of the Willkie 'One World' trip concerns the gift given to the man who was the United Kingdom's Ambassador to the USSR when the Willkie party reached Moscow, Lord Inverchapel (then Sir Archibald Clark Kerr). It occurred after they had left Moscow but Inverchapel told it himself to Willkie and Cowles when they met again in Washington after he was appointed Ambassador to the United States.

From time to time during countless years since I first heard it, I've had doubts about the story (despite having a letter to confirm it from Inverchapel's widow). However, recent corroboration came from Sir Frank Roberts who was then the British Minister, and Frank Giles who, as a Foreign Office attaché in Moscow, was also Inverchapel's private secretary. Now editor of the *Sunday Times*, he has himself written of the drama of the gift in very great detail in the newspaper in January 1980. Thirty years after the event, Giles had followed the trail and tracked it down to Scotland, where it is now a living legend.

That Inverchapel hadn't too much enthusiasm for the post where there were all too few of the sophisticated pleasures he normally enjoyed comes out in Harold Nicolson's *Diaries*, in which he wrote that the Ambassador wasn't sure about being named for the post in Moscow; in fact, he wasn't satisfied he was the right man for the job.

Although he got on well with Easterners, he had little opportunity to do so in Moscow – where, as he told Nicolson,

GIFT

he was followed by five detectives whenever he moved and not allowed to know anyone outside. Despite this concern, he left Russia with a unique personal gift from their awesome dictator.

Something which Stalin may have taken into account in choosing his gift was Willkie's story of how the Ambassador behaved at the banquet given in his (Willkie's) honour when he reached Moscow. Stalin singled Inverchapel out in an embarrassing and unwarranted tirade against Great Britain.

The War was at its peak. Despite the fact that the threatened siege of Moscow had been fended off, tension was still palpable; nevertheless, the banquet was replete with all possible trappings. Men wore full battle regalia and decorations. Food and drink, despite the difficulties, were more than ample.

Stalin's attack on the United Kingdom came like a bolt from the blue. After a few mellow words of welcome to Willkie, he became apoplectic, turning sharply away from his opening remarks by attacking the British, using Inverchapel as the whipping boy. Stalin's real target was Winston Churchill, whom he accused of personally causing the deaths of massive numbers of Russians by preventing aeroplanes and other American war supplies from getting to the USSR. (Stalin had obviously thought a great deal less of human life when he massacred millions of his own people in an unspeakable purge.)

Stalin continued to lash out, claiming that material from the United States intended for Russia had been sent on the precarious North Sea journey without sufficient convoys, that ships were lost, their material stolen, Russians slaughtered.

The shaken British Ambassador, though unprepared for such an outburst, nevertheless had the grace and skill to rise to the occasion. According to Willkie, he coolly reminded Stalin that the absence of suitable convoys was due to the terrifying loss of men and ships everywhere (many of them British) and to the magnitude of the Allies' needs on so *many* oceans; and that he was sorry to hear Stalin describe the lost war material as 'stolen'. 'Anything that isn't sorely needed to defend England comes to Russia,' he announced simply.

Even if Inverchapel's stamina had satisfied the old fox, as it probably did, he gave no sign that evening. Willkie tried to alleviate the tension by springing to his feet, raising his vodka and proposing a toast to Stalin. He then alluded to the brave British and particularly to Churchill's efforts, and ended up by stressing the quality of Stalin's leadership as well as the bravery and sacrifices of the Russian people. He also described the admiration of America's own President and the American people for Stalin personally and his countrymen's heroism (which he said he'd now seen for himself and would report to the nation back home).

All the others sprang to their feet to drink an exuberant toast to the tough, small man with the one short crippled arm. Stalin responded with a brief unsmiling nod. Noisy applause soon filled the hall; on the surface at least, anger had evaporated but Inverchapel must have left the dinner with a heavy heart.

Despite this shocking experience, Stalin never repeated his outburst again. Inverchapel and Stalin met without rancour and, when his four-year tour of duty came to an end in Moscow, Stalin gave the Ambassador the unprecedented honour of two farewells. One was a small dinner in the Kremlin with other members of the Embassy present; but the second, unique for Stalin, was one to which the Ambassador was invited alone, unattended except for Stalin's interpreter and Foreign Minister Molotov. According to Frank Giles's account of this meeting, no official record, no telegram, no word to the British Foreign Office exists. And this is rare.

Later, when Inverchapel told the story to Willkie, he said

GIFT

Stalin admitted how impressed he was by Inverchapel's behaviour at the banquet.

At the end of the last farewell dinner, Stalin remarked, 'You've been good to us. What would you like to take away as a suitable gift to remind you of Russia when you leave in a few days?' Inverchapel had been asked the same question at the first farewell dinner, but only replied jocularly, naming nothing except the four Russian girls who had married members of his British Military Commission who hoped to get unobtainable visas to leave Russia when their husbands returned to England (they got them as a result).

At the private, second dinner, when asked again what gift he'd like, the Ambassador smiled and quietly thanked Stalin, saying that his real gift was in taking away memories of the great Russian people and their leader.

Stalin was not put off by this *politesse*. 'There must be something you particularly like here and I'd like to give it to you,' he insisted.

Inverchapel replied, 'I remember, most of all, the people here. I will never forget them, their kindness to me; my staff, my valet. . . Would you be willing to part with this one Russian?' he asked jokingly.

In those days, by such a slip of the tongue, a man might have been condemned to death merely by having been singled out by a foreigner. Had the man been friendly to a foreigner, and why? Would the OGPU hear of it? Inverchapel told Willkie how deeply concerned he was after naming the man and how hard he tried to camouflage any special interest in him.

The man was Inverchapel's valet, Evgeni Yost, whom he employed at the Embassy as a servant and masseur and whom he'd have liked to keep on his staff. In a moment of regret, he went on:

'All the Russians I have ever met are remarkable; *everyone* is brave. No one in particular stands out. I shall go away remembering each man, woman and child I have ever met or seen in the streets. That is the gift I wish to take with me, nothing more.'

Thanking Stalin profusely for his flattering friendship, he left the Kremlin.

Two days later, he arrived at the airport to fly home to London, when his gift was presented to him. There the twenty-four-year-old Volga-German stood, looking ridicu-lous in a too-long overcoat and hat, ready to board the plane with him, acting as if it was the most normal thing in the world to be given away like a slave to another man – a human being, like a chattel, the object of an exchange between Stalin and a foreign diplomat. Inverchapel even spoke of having been given a scroll indenturing the man to him for life.

Lord Inverchapel is dead but the still stateless Evgeni Yost lives in Scotland, where he is married to a Scottish wife and has settled into an expensive stately Scottish home.

He is now a prosperous business man, dealing in fish and chips – and voting Conservative.

THE CAT CALLED

In a small flat, in London, a forlorn woman sat, very sad. Her constant companion for the last eight years lay in her basket, dead. Alone in her shabby bed-sitting room in Earls Court, she pondered on the best and most reverent way to bury Marmalade, the cat.

It had to be a proper burial, but the crowded block of flats had no garden. The Central London parks were too public, too populated. The answer came to her: somewhere in the green world of the heights above London called Hampstead Heath.

The body was wrapped in several brown paper bags. The small shovel, which ordinarily ornamented the gas-lit fireplace, was put into her shabby shopping hold-all. Stifling a tear, with her parcel in her left hand and the shopping bag in her right, she made her way to the nearest tube-station and bought a ticket to Hampstead.

The late autumn day was lovely; the air was soft and the sky was bright in the twilight. But for the sad occasion, she would have greatly enjoyed the walk across the green Heath in the cool air. At last she found the perfect place – a patch of bare

MARMALADE

earth near the trunk of a tree, where the grass refused to grow.

Three times she took out her shovel to scratch a shallow grave and three times passers-by stopped to watch her doing so. Again, stifling tears, this time of frustration, she knew the task was hopeless. Picking up her two bundles, she entrained homeward for Earls Court.

Someone had left a newspaper on her seat in the underground train and she read it to take her mind from her difficulties, piling the two packages on the seat next to her as the train got more crowded. Travellers came and went.

By the time she returned home, she felt weary and hopeless. Regretfully, she knew there was only one thing to do – to give her beloved cat to the caretaker to cremate in the large basement boiler.

However, before doing this, she could not suppress a sudden strong desire for one last look at Marmalade, her faithful friend.

With trembling fingers, she unrolled the brown paper package and nearly fainted as she drew from it a large, very pink, very fresh leg of lamb.

A second generation English dealer in 'antiques' in a low middle-class area of Paris is a rare bird indeed – but he did exist, and a great friend of mine, Enrico Donati, knew him. A steady flow of traffic used to pass this dealer's door on its way to the centre of the city and from it came an occasional sale. But mainly, his business was with the locals, selling hand-me-down second-hand beds and dining tables and the odd extra chair. Sometimes, people came to sell when they were without money.

He was the neighbourhood's principal 'bank' as well as their outlet. He knew everyone around him – their jobs, their ups and downs, their ability to pay. Making a hard bargain seemed his only zest in life; he was, in fact, a transplanted Scrooge in a strange land, speaking in a strange tongue. Goods were exchanged on a pre-First World War credit system of his own invention – one that would be frowned on in our pay-as-you-earn world today. Barter was not excluded. The man was needed but he was the enemy and not the friend. All the locals knew him and almost all hated him.

A more incongruous life for an expatriate Englishman simply could not exist; nor did anyone seem to remember how, when or why his father made the move across the rough Channel to settle amid the *petit bourgeois*.

Enrico Donati vouches for the authenticity of this story: one day, a young father of four children came in to the dealer with a piece of paper for sale. The purpose and plan of his visit had been widely discussed by a small group of friends who

FOR SALE

had been seeking for years for a way to extract revenge – to 'do the dealer in' as they had been done. Finally, this late afternoon, Michel, after a quick beer, excitedly hit on an idea. Loud hurrahs greeted the plan. He went off to a round of applause and all awaited his return from the dealer.

'I have something to sell you – but the price is high,' boasted Michel to the dealer. 'It is on this piece of paper – and it will cost you a lot of money.'

The amount, written down, was a fortune to anyone at that time – and Michel waited with glazed eyes while the piece of paper was examined.

It read: MY SOUL IS FOR SALE. THE PRICE IS 5,000 francs.

'*Parfait!* I will buy it!' responded the dealer. 'Here is your 5,000 francs.'

The whole transaction was over and done with in a few minutes. A stunned Michel walked out of the shop slowly, money in hand. The dealer did not call him back. It was true. He had 5,000 francs.

At last his wits returned. Jubilant, he raced back to the bar. At long last someone had outwitted the old Scrooge, and with real money, too – not just with a slip of paper and a credit!

The victory made news that spread throughout the neighbourhood like a grass fire; everyone was excited; everyone cheered Michel. People salved their own wounds by gloating over how Michel had tricked a man who had always had the upper hand. A hero was born.

The next day, people would talk of nothing else. In his own home, Michel was a god. His children suddenly saw father as a tall genius. His wife was bursting with pride, both were full of ideas about what to do with 5,000 francs.

Twenty-four hours later, Michel came back to the house and found an ominous silence in the sparse flat; his wife was white with concern.

'What have you done? You've sold something you don't own!' she burst out.

Michel almost collapsed. 'What is wrong with you; you must be mad!' he yelled back.

'No. I'm not mad. *You* are. The priest has sent word that you may never again step inside the church. You dared to sell God's gift for money. . .' she sobbed.

'But the priest simply could not be on the dealer's side,' Michel pointed out. He tried to reason with his wife that it was the dealer who was really the evil one.

'Don't worry. I will go and see Father François and explain it all to him. He won't be angry for long,' he said.

Before eating, Michel fled to his parish church and begged for an immediate audience with the priest. At first, the stern man was not even prepared to discuss the matter but finally he received Michel – only to confirm the fact that he was no longer welcome in the church.

Michel returned to an unhappy wife, and a terrible evening of silence. He didn't dare face his neighbours and for once he did not go out for his regular beer to the local saloon. His children were bewildered and sad.

The next day, he returned to a much more unhappy household – and, by this time, the word seemed to have passed through the neighbourhood too. People turned away, pretending not to see him, to avoid meeting his eyes or to talk. 'What now?' he could only ask himself.

Once inside his home, he heard the next piece of bad news. The children, who had been the 'one-day wonders' of their school, basking in their father's reflected glory, were now outcasts. The other pupils weren't even talking to them any more. Teachers had joined the priest in preaching to everyone the wickedness of his act. 'No man has a right to sell his soul,' even schoolchildren were saying, mimicking their elders.

His wife got a cool reception at the market. Neighbours turned away in the embarrassment which, in a week's time, was to become a noisy silence. The family soon found themselves ostracized.

Buy back your soul, or we won't be able to talk to you again, they seemed to be saying with every averted glance, every direct snub. And Michel, sleepless, unhappy, turned upon by every member of his household, knew this was his only course.

Not a sou of the 5,000 francs had been touched. The money lay on a bureau-table – too dangerous to need to be locked away. Finally, Michel picked it up on a hot, late day and took it back to the dealer, with a heavy heart and a heavy step.

'Here is your 5,000 francs back; I wish to buy back my soul,' he announced as he walked in the door.

'I'm sorry, but I don't wish to sell it now. I'm not interested,' the dealer replied.

Astonished, bowled-over by the unexpected reaction, Michel pleaded with the *antiquaire* – but to no avail. An anguished, vanquished man left the shop. In despair, every night, for ten nights he went back to try to change the dealer's mind. Each time, he left defeated, to return to a completely demoralized household. The repurchase had become everything in his life.

Michel's work suffered. He couldn't sleep. His wife was almost ill; the children dreaded school. Two Sundays had been agonizing to the family who (minus father) had to brave the friendless atmosphere of church and the unforgiving priest.

Finally, a desperate Michel rushed to the shop-keeper with a final offer: 'Either you sell me back my soul, or I commit suicide.'

'Very well,' replied the stony-faced man. 'I will sell; but my price has gone up, it will cost you 10,000 francs.'

TELEPHONE

This is a very short short story, about an elegant friend of our family who was once a member of the British government. He was so understated, so unaggressive that even his close friends constantly looked for visible evidence of the hard spine required to obtain and hold a post in the prevailing government's Cabinet. I quite naturally shall not reveal his identity.

He was soft-spoken, even gentle; he never raised his voice. He even allowed amateurs to deliver sweeping, inaccurate statements about his particular department's speciality, without making the slightest change in his calm demeanour. More than once, in awe of such detachment, I had to curb my irritation: why so indifferent, I often wondered.

He was widely known as a charming, kind person, also a little weak – but with many other disarmingly attractive characteristics. Although my husband and I knew him well enough to include him for Christmas in our Sussex house party, we knew very little about his family except that he lived alone and that his grown-up children had flown the nest and lived their lives somewhere far outside London. There couldn't have been many family ties as his free weekends were generally spent with friends. Questions weren't asked; his solo existence was taken as a matter of course.

A telephone call instantly changed all my views of him – in a bare few seconds of talk: I called him one day to ask what time to expect him the coming weekend. I dialled the usual private, unlisted number, heard the buzz, buzz of the tone, and suddenly he was there.

CALL

But he was talking to someone else. I had been accidentally plugged in to his engaged line, a trick of fate not unique in the telephone system.

'Hang up,' I kept telling myself. But there was something about the way that soft voice rose and fell (as I'd never before heard it do) that glued me to the phone. The nice man was a brute, attempting to put off a woman who was obviously quite a lot older. Here, in fact, was the arrogance and cruelty he kept so secret from his friends.

The woman, it soon became obvious, was his mother, sobbing through a flood of tears.

'. . . but I simply cannot get by on the few pounds you give me each week,' she cried. 'I am desperate.'

'That is all you're getting. Not a cent more,' he announced. 'You know I haven't all that much myself – and I've got quite a front to keep up. I'm tired of your nagging. This has simply got to stop!'

'Please don't say that,' she begged. 'I don't nag you, I rarely call. I stay out of your way – but I cannot possibly make ends meet on a few pounds a week.'

In those few moments of conversation, a picture emerged of a man with two natures – one for the public, the other in private – whose mother (or someone with an old woman's voice whom he was inadequately supporting) was a tragic figure. Someone who was apparently leading a lonely and unhappy life to enable him to keep up the fiction of his public life. My mind raced with rage.

By then, I was chained to the phone, having quashed the impulse to hang up, to take the receiver from my ear and put it back on its base, where it belonged. I felt that I must cut in, must let him know that by mistake I'd heard their conversation. I even had the impulse to say I'd make up the necessary money for his mother! I longed to denounce him.

If I had hung up, his personal reputation would have been ruined. How would I have known that the man I listened to merely appeared to have the same voice? This was not my friend; the woman called him John and the moment she did I realized, in a cold sweat, that this was a case of mistaken identity. I had dialled-in on the conversation of a stranger with a voice identical to the Cabinet Minister's.

If I'd done the proper thing and hung up after hearing just a short bit of their nasty conversation, I'd have loathed that nice man, for the wrong reason, for the rest of my life.

By doing the wrong thing, by staying on long enough, I realized I was listening to a stranger.

KOREAN

Journalism took me to many places but I'd like especially to tell of the Korean war front and of the Panmunjom Truce Conference. Few things I've seen in my life have been more beautiful than the view of the site where men were attempting to establish peace between the North Koreans and the Allied forces. The small area called Panmunjom buzzed with life. It lay in a protected area between the battleground of the ROKS and the Allies, headlined in the news for years – chiefly because it took place inside conference tents, frustrating the peaceful intentions of the Allied Command.

The Korean War had begun about four in the morning on 25 June 1950 – when 150,000 communist North Koreans, equipped with Soviet tanks and automatic weapons, suddenly crossed the thirty-eighth parallel and ruthlessly invaded South Korea – a stunning surprise. No one – either in the Land of the Rising Sun or in Washington – expected it. Nor did General MacArthur, if John Gunther's account of the General's movements on that very night in Japan is true. He had apparently accompanied the Gunthers when they went on his private train on a visit to Kyoto, and was deeply shocked, according to John Gunther (who was on an assignment to write an 'Inside Japan' for *Look* magazine), to hear on the train that shooting had begun in Korea.

When I got there in the January of 1953, it was almost two years to the day since the peace negotiations had begun. These started in Kaesong, but had to move to Panmunjom when the original site could no longer be protected from communist

WAR FRONT

fire. The weary scepticism at the opening of these talks finally led to a loud sigh of relief which was heard around the globe when the truce was eventually signed thirty long months later.

How did I get up to the front? President Eisenhower arranged for Mike Cowles and me to go. The request, made enthusiastically, lay heavily on my mind after the classified briefing given in Tokyo by General Matt Ridgeway's Command Headquarters, especially after being instructed on how to behave if captured. When I was finally fitted out in men's battledress (five layers) to cope with the twenty degrees below zero out there, my dislike of intense cold added to the jitters. I wanted, of course, to be intrepid – but I did once yearn (for a fleeting moment) for a terse order, rescinding the trip. . .

General Ridgeway very generously lent us his own personal plane for the trip to Seoul, a bomber with a non-existent heating system. My teeth never stopped chattering. The little hotplate aboard was not working so we were given ice-cold cocoa 'to keep us warm' by a kind-hearted young airman.

The manner of the air force officer in charge of the plane was very different; to him, a woman was an idiot to ask to go up to the front and the General was an even bigger one for allowing it. You could sense his contempt. I felt as if a block of ice was strapped to me when he came back and thrust a parachute into my lap, barking out, 'Here. Put it on. You may need it!'

'I don't jump,' I explained meekly as I put it on the seat

across the aisle. Mike Cowles's face was wreathed in a slightly nervous grin by then, but he didn't waste any time stepping into his.

'Do as I say. Put it on,' the captain snapped back. 'I'm in command here and you're under orders. If need be, we'll push you out!' he barked, brooking no nonsense.

So, without choice, I put the hideous object around me. The parachute, which doubled me up (adding cramp to coldness), was finally hooked on and I returned to my seat with my stomach turning over. The plane was constantly bombarded by pellets of ice flying off our wings. Each sharp rap, I was sure, was enemy fire (which, in point of fact, might have been less dangerous than icing up). Below, the sight of the snow-capped jagged hills was Martian. As we flew over them, regret kept bubbling to the surface. That horrible terrain was hell for soldiers to fight over. It was hell to contemplate landing on it by parachute.

Bivouacking with the officers was the next experience. Everyone slept on bunks in their dormitory; I was merely one new person, unrecognizably female. Toilet facilities then (and from then on) were a nightmare problem in a world where only men existed. Five layers of battledress were an added personal hazard.

Driving up to the peace talks at Panmunjom had been arranged by General Ridgeway. We were to go up with the men in the morning, so we rose early to clamber into the jeeps to ride up through the front. I was so disguised that only the most observant suspected a woman had arrived.

The horseshoe-shaped no-man's-land, almost encircled by communist troops fighting behind the thirty-eighth parallel to the north, was once a trysting place for lovers who will probably never use it this way again. When I went out there, all but a small gap to the south-east was held by communist forces. Five decrepit huts still stood where the original hamlet was located, and women and tiny children still lived inside them, ignoring the war. Nowhere ever looked less habitable.

A huge area had been marked off in the low flat ground between two mountains. Inside it, men were safe from the action which continued to take place above and around the zone. On both sides, armies were entrenched in jagged, high hills, lobbing their heavy artillery through the skies above the peace talks. When I was there, beneath them, it took me a long time to accept that thought casually.

To get there, men from each side followed a daily ritual, from which no one deviated, not by a moment nor by a move. When I once by mistake put a foot outside the outlined truce area instant machine-gun fire from men whose placements I could actually see, warned me to hop back. I did, like a scared rabbit.

Each morning at nine sharp, a moratorium was declared for ten minutes. In this period, the flutter of action was like a ballet, and just as precise. Men in jeeps and in planes descended like bugs, from both sides of the mountain, scurrying to the tents on the plain to take up their daily monotonous stations in the war of nerves across tables.

After ten minutes the shelling started again, but everyone who had scrambled through was safe until the time came to disband the conference. Again the ritual was repeated to allow all to dash out again for the night. If you were a military observer, you went back by jeep each evening to Seoul; a shell could always get you on the roads. If you were Press, you drove back to the cold, cramped railway-carriages parked outside Seoul, your home for the duration. About thirty war correspondents travelled back and forth daily with the officials at the truce-tables. Even those nerve-testing hours were a respite from the war.

The truce plain, when I first saw it from the front seat of an army jeep, which had bumped its way up from Seoul, looked indescribably lovely as we huddled by the side of the road, awaiting the signal for firing to stop so we could drive on.

I thought of Braque then, and I still do. The colours of the terrain, the markings on it, the tents and equipment would have done justice to his palette. The land was mustard green and puce. The area was marked off with devastating casualness by four narrow strips of cerise plastic, laid on the earth and held down by stones. From each of their corners (to mark the area from air-attack) helium-filled barrage-balloons were anchored – waving joyously in the sky overhead. These were silver. At night, four searchlights threw beams into the sky to define their glitter.

The truce tents, looking like blobs on a Cubist's palette, were either of dark brown, white, or black canvas. When

53

khaki and black jeeps and khaki and navy planes composed themselves in tight little groups alongside them, each added superbly to the Cubist composition. The colouring certainly was pure Braque.

Panmunjom's truce area itself was thick with languages; being a linguist was a very special luxury. Apart from the delegates, the press corps was a large UN in itself: Americans, French, British and South Koreans mingling with Japanese. On the other side was the communist contingent.

Fraternization between Press on both sides did take place – but only gingerly, being openly frowned on by the communists. Propaganda was constantly handed out by communists over the conference tables. Whenever this happened inside the tent, the Allied delegation tended to get up and leave the table. When meetings ended normally, the communist delegates just got up and walked out in a stiff procession – never relaxing their frozen expressions.

Wind tore inside the weather-beaten tents (warmed with electricity furnished by Americans). There, the team of five Allies faced a team of five communists across a narrow table. Despite the most unfriendly manner of these meetings, all men knew that world peace was involved in their discussions.

WAR FRONT

Six months after I left in January 1953, they succeeded in signing the truce.

I never think of Korea without recalling the story of Secretary of War Frank Pace's visit to the front lines there. He was inspecting evacuation procedures for the wounded which were remarkable. A mobile surgical unit reached men very promptly after injury; first-aid care was quickly given; helicopters then brought the wounded back to Seoul, where hospital attention was ready. Some intensive-care cases were flown to Tokyo, others back to the USA.

While talking to the wounded just brought back from the front lines, Secretary Pace bent over a badly wounded, dark-moustachioed soldier, who was lying on the ground utterly silent and calm. 'Don't worry. We'll soon get you to hospital in Tokyo,' he promised.

With a look of downright contempt, the man grabbed the curved surgical needle from the hands of a field-doctor working on him. Without a second's hesitation, he plunged the needle through his palm – in one side and out through the back of his hand!

'Me Turk. Me no hurt,' he growled back at the shattered Secretary of War.

ONE LARGE BLACK SPIDER

It took one black hairy spider to destroy the weekend life of a rich and famous New York couple.

Both worked very hard and were in search of the sort of weekend retreat in which they could completely unwind after rather frenetic weekday activities – and, they hoped, away from the social pattern of the city's cocktail-hour Connecticut and Long Island circuit. Though they had been commuting to Southampton, they wanted a less popular hideaway which would guarantee peace, contrast and beauty.

They found this elusive Nirvana entirely by accident in an island of the West Indies in the late forties – in an island where a calm atmosphere reflected the aftermath of the war years. Money was still frozen, neither tourists nor their agencies had begun to pounce on it; there wasn't time for the island's simple life even to start to change. One still heard the clop, clop of horses' hooves as they pulled carriages through the once-narrow winding lanes and little else but this cheerful sound and the occasional echo of calypso music drifting through the night marred the stillness. There was only the large hotel and not even a suspicion of the discotheques which eventually came to conquer the peacefulness. Roads were uncrowded; the few cars were rare. Even a passing carriage was only an occasional happening. Race relations were still good.

Although hardly considered the 'in' place at that time and not chic by ordinary sophisticated standards, the island had much else to commend it: it was not thick with houses and

AND ONE SMALL RABBIT

those that were there had simple architecture (strikingly painted in vivid pastels if not in dead white). For enthusiasts the vegetation was rich and plentiful. The sand was coral, crisp and clean. So was the sea – *clean*. Only a vague threat of hurricanes intruded on the island's tranquillity but as no one seemed to worry, no one passed this worry on to visitors. One regulation was an obvious reminder; a law was passed to keep down the quantity of glass used in windows.

It never occurred to either of the two New Yorkers to look to this place for their retreat. They only went there for a short holiday – very much on impulse and somewhat reluctantly on the advice of a friend who recommended a small club-hotel he knew, where they could remain alone in an adjoining cottage.

'There, believe me, you will be unnoticed; unbothered and unimportant,' he promised.

He was right; until, somehow, it did become known to the island's main families that the couple were visiting the club. Invitations to do all the things they came away to escape from began to arrive, only to be courteously declined except for one on the day before they were leaving. It was hard to resist the blandishments of a very nice gentleman who wished merely to show them the island. 'We have great variety here, and you should see it all,' he pointed out.

As promised, the trip was most enjoyable, ending with tea at the newly-built home of his widowed sister, whose pride in it was boundless. At that house they met their first moment of drama during the otherwise conventional holiday. Driving up, they came to a seemingly ordinary white-washed stone house. The excitement only began the instant the door was opened – revealing an astonishing vista.

Somehow (probably through family connections) the regulation concerning minimal use of glass had been by-passed. Looking through the doorway, they knew at once that this was not 'just another house'. There, before their eyes, was a complete wall of glass; on the other side of it miles and miles of blue sea and a remote horizon.

The house was perched on high across the end of a horseshoe cliff; below, down what seemed like hundreds of steps, was a private beach. The two arms of the cliff were wide and long but the house had been constructed in such a way that they could only be seen after walking outside to the stone terrace which connected them to the house. Inside, impeccably furnished by its designer, it was sparse but beautiful.

On the left arm of the cliff, a guest house had been added; it too was almost out of sight and an exact copy in miniature of the ground floor of the main house: only a large bedroom, a bath and kitchenette. Altogether, the little estate was irresistible.

'This is it! We must get it somehow,' was the thought that raced through the wife's mind. Both she and her husband had been equally struck by its location (well off the main road), by its architecture (by an inventive New York stage designer), by its strange beauty and its size – small but impressive.

Though eminently desirable, it was obviously unavailable. Yet, quite undaunted, the two began to persuade the at first shocked, then angry and, finally, the intrigued woman owner. Eventually, just before leaving the island, it was their possession – by means known only to the three of them. Could it have been, as rumoured, the lure of a year in New York, paid for in post-war dollars? Whatever the bait, in the end the woman gave up her beautiful new toy and the New Yorkers began to commute to the island.

A ritual was established: the two went to work especially early on Friday mornings, did their dictation and tended to matters at hand and then, comfortably and without rush, boarded a noonday plane twenty minutes away from their offices at New York's La Guardia Airport. After lunch, they landed on the island, having taken no more time (and possibly less) than it would have taken to drive behind thick traffic every Friday to a Southampton beach house. From early afternoon until they boarded the nine o'clock evening plane on Sunday, they spent three days away from it all.

They decided to live in the guest house. Its glass frontage faced the rising sun but this fact was balanced by its being removed from any and all sounds in the main house – such as the staff's early arrival, breakfast being prepared, dusting being done. The occasional pair of guests, who were flown down by them on Fridays, were given the master suite in the big house. It wasn't noisy as we understand noise today but it lacked the dead silence of the guest house. Meanwhile, the blackest of black-out curtains were drawn across the wall of glass in that house before putting out the lights at night. The rising sun was no longer a problem.

A blow descended some months later, in May. From that time until October it seemed to the wife that the island belonged to insects. Spiders, totally harmless but large, sharply defined and long-legged, became sudden black patches on white-washed walls, worse when indoors. The sight of just one would produce hysteria in her. Fat black beetles plonked down loudly as they crash-landed on stone floors at night, attracted by lights. Flying cockroaches, the scourge of both tropical and southern towns everywhere on earth today, seemed to lurk by the hundreds, particularly in the hedges bordering the terrace – from which they flew out as the sun disappeared. These were inches long.

For anyone distressed by all creepy-crawlies, as she was, the experience was terrifying – even more so since neither her husband nor guests seemed to mind their presence. Each insect unnerved her, but spiders in particular became an obsession. Life became intolerable as soon as the sun set. Weekends lost their enticement. Instead of enjoying the beauty of the night while sitting outside, she began to dread the approach of evening. This first amused and then annoyed everyone around her, especially her hysteria when any one of the flying objects landed on her arm or hair.

One night in bed in their darkened room, black-out curtains drawn, the room silent, she woke her husband in great distress.

'There's a very large spider on the ceiling above us,' she

cried out. 'I know it. I feel it.'

'You must be mad! There's no way you could possibly see anything in this pitch-black room. How could you know there's a spider above us?' her husband responded in anger as he snapped on the light.

There *was* a spider on the ceiling – directly above her head! She nearly fainted. She dressed, waited anxiously for daylight to arrive, took the first plane bound for New York. And never again returned to that island.

Another story in striking contrast, concerns a small country rabbit caught up in a war.

One of the things I like about the British is that, despite the importance it played in their lives, they rarely do discuss the War. But my husband and I love this story, told to us by a relative of the soldier involved.

A small tank battle during the latter stages of the Second World War in Belgium had lasted about two days when the Germans decided to withdraw, and the British tanks took up the position they vacated. The officer involved, although very tired, inspected his new surroundings from the turret of his tank.

AND ONE SMALL RABBIT

Being a countryman, he was surprised and somewhat pleased to see a rabbit in a hutch against the wall of a battered farmhouse. In spite of the battle, although the rabbit appeared to be in splendid health, the British officer knew that it couldn't have had much food.

He jumped down from the tank, collected the rabbit and slipped back inside the turret with the soft creature in his arms – to feed him a few dry biscuits. He then realized that what he needed most after nights of battle was sleep. Standing up in his small area, he fell asleep. It was fitful, more an unconscious doze than a sleep, during which he felt a pulling and a tugging at his right arm.

His first coherent thought was the sound of his Colonel's voice, calling his name. Immediately awake, he was out like a flash on the ground, saluting his Colonel – whose first words were a stuttered, 'John, I didn't know you'd been wounded!'

His right sleeve was torn and the flesh lacerated around the elbow. It seemed absurd to tell the Colonel that he was not wounded but had only been bitten by a rabbit, having just descended from a twenty-ton tank.

His silent courage was rewarded by a Medal for Valour. He ended the War with a splendid decoration which could never be discussed. Ten or fifteen years later, the bemused relative told the story to us in confidence, hence no names.

THEFT FROM

After the Second World War, one of America's more colourful heroes was General MacArthur. In the prime of his life, he led his men on the beaches against the Japanese, rescued the Philippines, presided as a 'Pro Consul' over defeated and demoralized post-war Japan and at the same time commanded the United States Army in Korea until he was dismissed in an historic incident by President Truman for his wilful refusal to obey orders from the White House to end that war at the thirty-eighth parallel.

The vanity which lay behind his much-photographed handsome profile was so obvious that even his ardent supporters had to face the problems of excusing it. Perhaps one of the best accounts of this flaw in his character is in a story which I first heard in the early fifties, many, many years after the event – told so often that it eventually wore thin and died, although it was never forgotten. If it was apocryphal I never heard it challenged.

The scene was West Point, America's military academy, located close to New York City. It was early in the young General's career, just after he'd been appointed to his first important command, in charge of the Academy. The house which went with this post was such a simple one, hardly acceptable to him, that a New York furniture shop was hired to do the redecoration. They turned it into what must have been a conventional suburban home, of which the General was monumentally proud.

When completed, Douglas MacArthur instituted a weekly

A GENERAL

stag luncheon to which a carefully selected cross-section of men of importance from New York City were invited: a banker, a lawyer, a councilman, a politician, or editor. He presided over his table with splendid skill, showing the earliest signs of his capacity to hold his audience, to make admirers of potentially useful citizens.

Incidentally, he put this talent to its most dramatic test after he was dismissed by Truman. In retaliation, he embarked immediately upon an ill-fated and badly-conceived campaign to defeat Truman in the election for the Presidency of the United States (which a very different General, Dwight D. Eisenhower, won instead). It was a short, demoralizing campaign – one of the first lost by the old warrior. He had mistaken his ticker-tape hero's welcome on the streets of New York City after his dismissal as a symbol of a country-wide popularity.

The luncheons at West Point must have been successful as they continued for a very long time but one custom must have diminished the success. After luncheon, the General led his guests around the house in what must surely have seemed to be an embarrassing house-proud tour – in a house somewhat less impressive than those in which most of his guests lived. The last stop was dramatic – his bedroom.

Pointing to a large double bed which had an expanse of grey velvet covering it as well as being the focus of attention, he asked: 'See that bed? Such a bed is not for me – I'm a field officer,' he said pounding his chest 'and I'd never sleep in that.

PERUVIAN PORTRAIT

Portrait of Inca Prince Garcelaso de la Vega

A WOMAN IN A TAXI

Fleur Cowles and General George C. Marshall
with Mrs Marshall (who took a wrong-way
taxi journey during the Coronation of Queen Elizabeth II)

KOREAN WAR FRONT

Fleur Cowles in battledress at Korean War front

A MASTERPIECE ON DEMAND

The 'Lace-Maker' by Vermeer,

A MASTERPIECE ON DEMAND

and its copy by Salvador Dali

A NEW FACE

The new face of Jacqueline Auriol, one of the
world's greatest pilots

THE BIRD MAN AND THREE TREES

Carl Wiseman, the 'bird man' of Denmark,
who made dogs sing

STALIN'S GIFT

Evgeni Yost, the subject of a story told by
Lord Inverchapel, former United Kingdom
Ambassador to the USSR

I'll show you where I *do* sleep' and, opening a door to what seemed to be no more than a large closet, they saw, crowded inside, a camp cot, a small wooden chair and a simple chest of drawers. 'This is my bed,' he boasted.

Some must have left the house in confusion, but every time they left, he retraced his walk, recalling with satisfaction what he had said at each step of the way, proud of some remarks and honing others for future use.

After one such luncheon attended by particularly important guests, he was standing alongside his living room fireplace, staring in shock at the mantelpiece. A salver, which had had pride of place, was gone! The sterling silver piece, inscribed by men important to him, had simply disappeared between the time he had passed it on the way to the dining room and some hours later when all had gone.

In a rage, he summoned his entire staff, mostly military, except for a civilian female cook. 'One of you is a thief. Which one of you took my silver salver?' he demanded. 'You might as well confess,' he insisted, 'or all of you will be charged and that fact will permanently appear on your records. Own up now and save the others from disgrace.'

A GENERAL

They were all appalled – and silent, until the shy cook suddenly broke into tears. 'I know exactly who took it,' she sobbed. 'It was one of your guests. I saw him quietly put it inside his jacket – and I can describe him perfectly for you.'

After she had given a complete description, he instantly recognized the man. Summarily dismissing the staff, he sat down to his desk and sent the guest a letter: 'A joke is a joke but I would like to have the return of my silver salver,' he wrote, maintaining as much calm and courtesy as he could in his fury.

Three weeks later he had still had no reply and, brooding with ever-increasing rage, wrote a second letter. 'A thief is a thief. I demand my silver salver back – and at once.'

The embattled guest had, in fact, been on a holiday on the West Coast, quite unaware of the correspondence from the General. Finding the two letters on his return, he responded immediately. 'Dear General MacArthur, if you were not such a goddamn liar, you'd have found that silver tray by now between the sheets in that cot in which you are supposed to sleep.'

It took three years of odd research before I could write *The Case of Salvador Dali*, which was authorized by Dali himself. I'd read the literature by and about the eccentric surrealist painter, and heard endless stories from him in his special kind of Catalan-Spanish-English.

He gave me the necessary collaboration and when the manuscript was written (every page of which he was asked to initial before publication) the egocentric gentleman called it a *'monument historique'* and referred journalists to me for a long time after with 'Fleur Cowles knows more about me than I do.'

I had no history to reflect upon. There was just the living man and his living record to look straight in the eye. I decided he simply couldn't be taken at his word; not believing his stories, I went all over Europe to interview his teachers and fellow-students, family, fellow-painters, friends – finally, his psychoanalyst – only to discover, to my ever-increasing surprise if not horror, that his often unbelievable, sometimes perverted, sometimes ghoulish, sometimes hilarious stories were all true!

I wrote the book in three parts: 'The Man', 'The Genius' and 'The Paranoiac'. In 'The Man', I discussed his wild Catalan background and his Russian wife, Gala, the mysterious woman who saved him from insanity and eventually married him, thus taking over his life in many ways; his years in the teeming Paris of the thirties then in the US; his personality which ranged from gentle to sadistic in his youth to the manically devoted husband who became devoutly

SALVADOR DALI

religious, and to the reveller in tawdry sensationalism.

In 'The Genius', I discussed his other talents, besides painting – from set designer, to showman, to scenarist, to inventor, to mystic, to astronomer, to poet, to Cellini-like jewellery designer to the splendidly hair-raising author (particularly of the novel *Hidden Faces*).

In 'The Paranoiac', I took the known clinical facts about him and coupled them with my own informed surmises. I catalogued the meanings of such Dali symbols as his limp watches, lobster-telephones, crutches, elephants on stilts, and ended the book with a glossary of surrealist terms, all gleaned from his own quotations.

The paranoiac, I must explain in scientific terms, is in a normal state of health; there is no need to look for organic disorders. Yet the paranoiac lives and acts in a world apart from and different from the one we call normal. This is Dali in a nutshell, an isolated phenomenon.

He once pointed out to Mike Wallace in a slice of a dizzying television programme on WABC in New York, 'You see, my kind of craziness is a craziness of precision.' Other times he'd remind me regularly that the only difference between him and a madman was that he, Dali, was not mad; at other times he boasted of madness, claiming to be a madman. The result is that the world takes him at his own word. 'Madman' fell off typewriter keys in press rooms, from lips in drawing rooms and, more seriously, from the pens of art critics.

To me the essential difference between a madman and an

artist is that the madman never manages to impose his own vision of the world on others, while the artist does. Dali's behaviour gets in the way of objective appraisal, other than when he is considered as a leading figure of the early surrealist movement – and that was many decades ago.

Recently he was finally given the yearned-for accolade of a retrospective exhibition at the Beaubourg Centre, in Paris and in the Tate Gallery, in London. Continuing recognition will certainly follow. However, even in the years when he was considered a publicity-mad exhibitionist, a connoisseur and collector such as Chester Dale had nothing but admiration for Dali in the early fifties – as a man and as an artist. But, the greatest individual tribute to him as a painter has been paid by A. Reynolds Morse of Ohio who for so many years fought a one-man battle for serious recognition of Dali's worth. In his own museum in St Petersburg, Florida he has more Dalis than anywhere else in the world – hundreds of oil paintings, drawings, prints, water colours, ties, scarves, fabrics and numerous pieces of his jewellery. One is tempted to ask if the Morses have never awakened to a 'Dali Hangover'.

The most unfriendly critic tends to concede that 'The Christ of St John of the Cross', now hanging in the Glasgow Art Gallery and Museum in Scotland, is a masterpiece. Dali painted it when Catholicism returned officially to his life and it may well rank alongside the finest religious paintings created. The man on the cross is depicted from above; one looks at him from a strange perspective which few painters could achieve.

When the painting was bought by the Glasgow Art Gallery and Museum for £8,000 the price caused a sensation, but if it was put up for sale today, one can only surmise the huge price it would fetch. Dali's true standing may have to wait to be decided after his death, when all the Dalinian shenanigans and outbursts are forgotten.

London was at one time the focal point of his artistic reputation. For at least two years in the early thirties, Dali had a private, exclusive, rich de Medici of his own, Edward James, who nurtured his work by paying him the money to live. James also indulged Dali by displaying such surrealist props as his first 'lobster-telephone' in his London home. In England Edward James not only collected the largest private group of

Dali's paintings, but was also responsible for introducing Dali's work to other influential collectors.

It was New York that Dali couldn't survive without. He soon called it his 'American Campaign', and promptly dubbed it 'An Immense Gothic Rocquefort Cheese'. Once he fell in love with the place, he developed a constant routine of life, spicing his quiet existence in Spain with esoteric, noisy forays into New York. He became a different man; the rigid figure who had sailed to America in a tiny stateroom well below the luxury decks of a giant ship in the early thirties chose the posh St Regis Hotel on Fifth Avenue as his permanent New York address. There, for five months of the year, a tiny bedroom became a crowded studio where he painted under the cramped and surrealistic conditions he relished. The hotel met all his strange conditions; it had snob appeal and it was close to good restaurants as well as being conveniently close to the homes of the rich he preferred. Somehow under such conditions, he actually painted daily in his tiny bedroom.

The rather grand Hotel Meurice in Paris gave him an equally odd situation in which to paint – and had the right kind of public foyer for the audiences with callers which he adored.

He continued to oscillate like a pendulum between his two lives – emerging from the relative obscurity of his home in Port Lligat, in Spain, to touch base with International Society as a Spanish Grandee. In New York he got the publicity he needed as a cloak to wrap around his inner sense of insecurity. When satiated by this, he craved the solitude he needed in the comparative loneliness of Port Lligat. Now he is ailing, old and very frail; a man born in 1904, dramatically gaunt and emaciated with shoulders and moustache drooping.

Port Lligat was once a no-man's-land, isolated and lonely, untravelled. It is now sadly an unrecognizable tourist haven. Dali was happiest in the days when someone was grand enough to arrive by yacht and drop anchor in the port below. For a guest to come by yacht was to bring one's own bedroom, removing the irksome thought of domestic arrangements for guests from Dali's or Gala's mind. One might dream of a luxurious bed in a Dali setting, with push-button surrealistic conveniences, but though such luxuries do exist, they are for the Dalis, with not one square foot in reserve for guests.

I was well aware of this before I went to visit him there in the fifties at the peak of his recklessness – when the port was still lonely and unvisited. He was working in the exotic atmosphere of the home he had created by the gradual addition of fishermen's huts. There were five of them in all which he and Gala turned into a setting that would do justice to a surrealistic movie.

Writing the book, it was essential for me to see the brooding atmosphere of Port Lligat which Dali used to describe – the mysterious quality at night, the black light, the mystical rooms around him – all of which influenced his mind and his work. And I knew, of a certainty, that the visit would have its measure of nonsense.

George Bernard Shaw once told H.G. Wells that every historical personality – in fact every person of importance – could be characterized by three carefully chosen anecdotes. My visit to Port Lligat provided at least one.

'How do I get to Barcelona?' I asked Dali when we met in the foyer of the Ritz Hotel when both he and I were in Madrid.

'Very simple. Fly Barcelona. Then catch train to Cadaques. My secretary meet. Putch information telegram,' he ordered.

A few days later, I did as I was told but of course Dali had given bad advice. Either he should have sent a car to Barcelona to pick me up or suggest that I hire one. It took hours of waiting between leaving the plane and getting on the train, which was slow, crowded and hot. Surrealism set in when I arrived in Cadaques to discover there was then no road to Port Lligat. There was only a harsh and unmanageable path over rocks, although today it has been replaced by a road.

I wandered around; no one either saw or knew Dali's secretary. I decided to get to his house on my own, but the next hurdle was to find anyone willing to go there. The local taxi, owned by a very old man with a car of the same vintage as himself, refused to attempt the journey in the tired old vehicle. The lure of money, backed by American persistence, finally won and I stepped into the battered wreck.

As soon as we left the village behind, I understood his unwillingness. I too began to worry. The car could hardly cope with the potholes, crevices, rocks and the up-and-down hills. Would I (morally, if not technically) be responsible for his car?

The questions were soon resolved. The engine struggled, turned over and died at the foot of a particularly bad hill. The car had slipped and slipped backwards, a few yards at a time, before dying. I stopped a heart beat or two myself.

Decisions had to be taken quickly. I was wearing high-heeled shoes, not expecting to hike over rock-strewn hills. I had luggage to carry. And how could I leave the poor old man on his own with an unwilling car?

Suddenly, an incongruous figure appeared over the brow of the hill – a man on a Vespa scooter, shouting excitedly.

'Mais vous êtes trop tôt! Je suis le secretaire de Monsieur Dali. Bien venue!'

He was only two hours late, and had the gall to act as if I had come too soon. His beaming smile, waving my telegram in the air, was irritating.

After a few loud screams by secretary and taxi driver (in the Spanish I know now but didn't know then) the taxi driver was mollified. I was then invited to join the secretary on his scooter. Pushing a large bill in the taxi driver's hand, I climbed on a vehicle I had never mounted before.

I was hardly prepared. Somehow, we made it – with me straddling the seat with my dress pulled high, my black silk Dior coat floating behind, a suitcase in one hand and my handbag in the other. Having no hand free to cling to either scooter or driver, I could only pray.

We struggled up the first hill, magic alone keeping me on that seat. We navigated one hill only to face a low valley; up and down we jostled for an interminable time, often missing one large rock in order to jolt up against another.

Finally, over a longish hill, I saw the exquisite little port of Lligat below (as I like to remember it, an almost empty cove). There was the incredibly beautiful harbour he'd described, and there Dali was standing nearby in strange clothes – posing as if for some strange tableau.

The scooter skidded to a halt. I fell off, landing on a pile of jagged stones, everything I owned scattered around me. When I was helped by the secretary to my feet, one leg was bleeding profusely, my skirt torn, my clothes a mess.

None of this seemed to worry Dali. There was no sign of

concern or regret or embarrassment. The sight of blood, my appearance and my despair merely delighted the man. Grinning from ear to ear, he cried out joyously:

'Wonderful! Wonderful! Thank you! Very Dalinian arrival!'

I had outdone the madman on his own territory.

NORTH AFRICAN

The central characters in this story may still exist, so I have confused their identities by disguising their descriptions and changing all the locations involved – should they wish no further celebrity than they've already earned (all of it tragic to their families). The story is well-known, however, by those who live near them.

It begins with a stocky, middle-aged woman of ordinary mien disembarking from a luxury cruise at Algiers. Only three weeks before, she had left behind a lifetime of insular local existence. The ship was in port for two days to allow excursions into the hills outside.

She had boarded under protest, dreading the unfamiliar deck of a ship and yearning not to be separated from her husband and family. Despite all arguments the family doctor had decreed that only the sea air, preferably on board ship, would help her recuperate from a grave illness.

Her husband had never interrupted the day-to-day chores of his family bank in a small town in northern England and couldn't see his way to taking four weeks away from duty for such a trip. She had never been out of England and her starry-eyed, newly-married daughter couldn't be asked to leave with her after only a few weeks of marriage. After a conference of the tightly-knit family, Mother was persuaded to take off, alone.

The liner had already called in on many ports in many lands, after leaving Southampton, and by the time it reached Algiers she was quite another woman, having acquired the

ADVENTURE

lovely taste of independence and an awareness of her wealth – which, until now, neither she nor her husband had ever utilized. She soon began to live aboard ship at the same standard as the other rich passengers, on what was undoubtedly one of the most expensive liners in the world. As she swiftly regained health and dipped into her income, she realized untouched wells of extravagance. She began to enjoy her new self, and to buy more suitable clothes in every port.

When they reached Algiers, she had made up her mind not to join the others on the planned tours. She wanted to see the city on her own, to go to the main hotel and taste a little of her new-found freedom.

She rang for the steward and explained she wouldn't be joining the tour. She had already packed two bags to take for two days at the hotel recommended by the purser. 'Call me a porter to take my bags,' she requested, as she followed the steward down the gangplank after the others had gone.

A middle-aged Arab, smiling at her with a mouthful of gold teeth, awaited below and anxiously grabbed the two bags. He asked in good English where she was going.

'To the hotel,' she replied.

'If you haven't been in this city before, it is not too long a walk to the hotel, and I will gladly act as your guide,' he purred. 'We'd be going through the most fascinating part of our city. Why not walk?' he suggested.

The idea appealed. The two slowly wound their way to the hotel, everything en route being enthusiastically pointed out and explained. When they arrived at the hotel, the Arab porter, still with a bag in each hand, came into the hotel, standing alongside as she signed the register. An attempt by a hotel employee to take her and her bags to her room was repulsed by the insistent Arab, who carried her bags to her room himself. He never left.

The family was bewildered and concerned to be told a week later that she had left the ship before it steamed out of Algiers headed for South America. Bewilderment and concern turned to dismay and horror when cheques made out for large sums of money started flowing in at an alarmingly extravagant rate for her living expenses. All letters to her were unanswered.

After a few idyllic days in the hotel with her lover, she had moved into the palatial house she bought from an American expatriate who moved on to a new life elsewhere.

Her life there, according to new friends and neighbours, was less than ordinary. The native-garbed Arab already had a wife or two and many children, and they were all moved into the rear of the ground floor and back garden, often squatting and squabbling in the kitchen where they were cautioned in no soft terms to keep the peace. The chatter of Arabic continually punctuated the atmosphere.

Meanwhile, the family at home in northern England grew more stunned and helpless. Nothing must be said to anyone. A local scandal had to be avoided at any cost. All three, in any case, kept reassuring one another that Mother would come out of the incredible daze caused, they kept agreeing, by her illness and would return home. Meanwhile, not a soul was to suspect the truth.

Family friends clucked in dismay when they heard she'd suffered a slight relapse but was 'in good hands in the Argentine', where she was supposed to be when she took ill again. 'A sojourn in the warmer climate of a South American villa was just what she needed,' the family explained.

The final sign, which put paid to the notion of her return, came when cheques began to arrive signed in Arabic. They knew it would be difficult to intercept the post from Algiers every time it came. A family conference in which tears flowed and consternation was rife, was held. All kinds of suggestions were brooded over.

It was decided that someone had to go out and reason with

the woman – not a member of the family, but a trusted bank associate who would have to be taken into their confidence. He would remind her in an impersonal way of the difficulties and embarrassments back home. And it would be easier for her to return than if she were to lose face before a member of her family.

Accordingly, a somewhat timid and bewildered man was sent by air to Algiers, having agreed to undertake the mission under immense pressure, on the grounds of duty to the bank and friendship with the family. He loathed the idea, but went out of a sense of sympathy.

With embarrassment and trepidation, the small-town banker, indifferent to the heat of Africa, wearing the typical banker's dark suit and bowler hat descended on an imposing house in a strange country, to be ushered in by an Arab servant. He lost his nerve completely when confronted by the re-styled wife of his employer, who promptly showed him to the door with the message to take home that she intended to stay permanently.

That was the full extent of her conversation. He had said nothing and wasn't even able to open his brief-case to confront her with the collection of cheques that she and the Arab had made out in wilful extravagance. All he could report on his return was that she looked well (very well), that she had changed (considerably), that she was now even somewhat glamorous (her clothes, in particular), and that she lived lavishly – but that he had no opportunity even to glimpse the gentleman involved.

Dismay settled on the family. Once again, they invented a new ailment which was supposed to detain Mother. They realized that someone from the family must shortly go out to be with her. One couldn't keep the story going without explaining why no relative had gone out to her.

By all odds, it had to be the daughter who would have to confront her mother, to explain their terrible position and to bring her back home. Most reluctantly, the daughter left her new husband and took off under a carefully prepared plan of action.

Arriving in Algiers, she left the airport to go to the same hotel. The attractive young Arab taxi-driver who took her bags at the airport carried her bags into the hotel, then up to her room, and he never left.

All four now live in splendidly incongruous bliss in the big

ADVENTURE

house, which we visited when my husband and I went for a drink with local friends.

BASEMENT

My first book was published in 1951. Called *Bloody Precedent*, it was about two married couples who ruled in the Argentine with an iron will in exactly the same way as the Perons did later – using the same techniques and devices – not only having the same successes but sharing identical fates.

Juan and Encarnacion de Rosas, the original pair, had ruled (in fact terrorized) their country almost exactly one hundred years before their identical successors, Juan and Evita Peron, took over the same land. So alike were they that the Perons ordered the de Rosas' history to be banned; most of my research had to come from outside Argentina, much of it I found on library shelves in England.

One can only marvel at the historic coincidence:

(1) Manuel de Rosas was less tyrannical than his wife, so was Juan Peron. Both men left the cruel decisions to their wives, who made them with relish.

(2) Encarnacion, *not Evita*, invented the 'shirtless ones' (poor followers) for which Evita became famous. Encarnacion, not Evita, was the first to use it to appeal to the unhappy poor and all dissidents. Evita followed suit, using the same emotive terms.

(3) Like de Rosas, Peron had a finicky insistence on legalistic behaviour; Evita, like Encarnacion, was indifferent to it. Evita, an unexpected and unpredicted rival of her own husband, worked constantly to win the shirtless ones (the 'Descamisados') to her side. The poor learned to take their cue from her, not him. She was their drama, their make-believe,

STORY

their ego; she was glamorous while they were shabby but she seduced them, as Encarnacion had done before her, by false promises.

(4)　Long before the Perons took over the press of their country, the de Rosas had done it.

(5)　Photographs of Encarnacion and Juan Manuel were obligatory everywhere; as were photographs of the Perons, except that Evita turned them out more profusely.

(6)　Both couples set every rule for living, speaking, writing, callously killing their opposition.

(7)　Encarnacion died of a mysterious disease of the stomach, probably cancer; Evita died of stomach cancer.

(8)　Juan Manuel fled for his life to England, alone. Juan Peron fled to Madrid (alone but for the rumoured covey of teenaged girls) and the ultimate company of Evita's successor, Isabelita.

I wrote my book somewhat under threat. The Perons didn't want that book published. I was warned; I eventually asked for and got protection – and the man sent from the Argentine to intimidate and frighten me was arrested and deported.

Apart from being declared *persona non grata* by the Perons, I had little or no idea what impact the book had back in the heavily-censored Argentine. I couldn't appreciate what it would mean to many there.

American press interest up to that time was relatively little. They seldom reported Evita as a political power: most of the time she was reviewed in the same terms as a movie star or a pop singer would be, and her considerable (mainly evil) effect on Argentina's history was largely ignored.

My book was the first one to take any serious note of the Perons and, quite unbeknown to me, I was automatically chosen as the ally of the anti-Peron underground movement as soon as it was published. In the United States, I was ultimately inundated with mail from Montevideo, taken there by Argentinians who swam across the River Plata at night to take the letters across to safety. A gallery of literary expatriates had developed; many used Montevideo as a refuge. Exiles ended their silence by working and writing there. Others risked their lives by swimming the river in darkness in order to speak freely. Montevideo was an extraordinary city, which held out its hands to the political and intellectual exiles from the Argentine, and it served anti-Peronists just as it had done the anti-Rosasists before.

I turned their voluminous coded and interpreted correspondence over to Allen Dulles, director of the CIA at the time, knowing no better use to make of it, and sent my book to every congressman and senator, hoping their awareness of the situation might help in some way.

Quite a large number of anti-Peronists were plotting their overthrow – and when they did, they used a very special basement as headquarters.

One hundred years before, the literary rebels who longed for the overthrow of de Rosas used the same basement of an insignificant book shop as their rendezvous. When de Rosas closed it, they promptly formed a retaliatory society, the *Associacion de Mayo* to restore a free government.

This was the same basement which was used one hundred years later by the anti-Peronists. The magic room also served as a meeting place to read my book – a page at a time torn from a copy which had been smuggled in. To be found with the book was treasonable. But there, under the shop, men and women read and discussed it and hatched their plot to oust Peron.

The book shop was owned by a woman who had fled from Nazi persecution and was obviously only too eager to offer the basement which had already served one revolution.

The two greatest women aeroplane pilots of our time were both Jacquelines: one, Jacqueline Cochran, the other an Auriol (daughter-in-law of the then President of France). I've known them both. For years, the hard-fought Harmon trophy for the greatest flying achievement every twelve months used to swing from one of these women to the other. Both heedlessly risked their lives in the air – and Jacqueline Auriol almost lost hers doing so.

In 1950, New York City's Dr John Marquise Converse, famed for his reconstructive plastic surgery, was invited to the Elysée Palace in Paris to examine Jacqueline Auriol's face. She had already undergone twenty-two operations to try to re-build the structure of her face but she was still severely disfigured, feeling so monstrous and so distraught over her appearance she wouldn't allow her two sons to see her. She was just over thirty, having been just as famous for her style and chic as the President of France's daughter-in-law as for her prowess in the air.

Undaunted by her terrible accident, she insisted that a miracle be found to make her face acceptable, that she must lead a normal life and that she must fly again. Her face had been smashed in a crash; she had been co-piloting a new hydroplane which suddenly nose-dived and plummeted into the Seine, and in the crash her face had been thrust against the instrument panel.

She was barely alive when pulled from the wreckage, a ravaged international beauty. The bone structure of her face

FACE

had been horribly broken and pushed forward. There were two hundred fractures. Her mouth and nose were smashed out of shape. Miraculously, her eyes escaped serious damage, but her face was gone.

At thirty-one, she joined the dark ranks of the facially mutilated. There are tens of thousands of these people in the United States alone – the result of burns, car accidents, mishaps at birth. They rarely appear in the daylight, working only at night, spending their time hiding their faces. Jacqueline Auriol's own description of the broken face was 'The face of a child without playmates, a man without a job, a woman who locks herself away from all her family – and shuns mirrors'.

Could Dr Converse make a new face after so many attempts? Could she ever again lead a normal life? He agreed to try. She was secretly moved under an alias to his own operating theatre in New York, where a trusted and remarkable crew was at hand. Heavily bandaged and with a false name, she came to the clinic. Because I had helped Dr Converse create the first clinic for the facially disfigured, in fact, the tiny precursor of the now immensely important reconstructive plastic surgery unit at NYC – Bellevue Hospital, of which Dr Converse was instigator, creator and head until his death in 1981 – I was called into the plot.

His superb skills were soon demonstrated. After a full day of surgery, the new face which had been re-designed from the one available was built and stitched into place. It didn't resemble her own face; there was no way in which it could. This was surgically immaterial. Instead of the rather acquiline French face, she now had a round, even happy one.

Not only a new face but a new personality emerged. Mme Auriol made a remarkable mental post-surgery recovery, often the hardest problem of all for such patients. As soon as her mind was relaxed and she had accepted her new face, the aviator in her was re-awakened. She insisted on flying again.

Under her assumed name (and between scar tissue removals) the world's greatest woman pilot went incognito to the Bell Aircraft Corporation in Buffalo, to learn to fly a helicopter. There, the late Laurence Bell, who ran the company (also one of the trustees of our hospital) put a helicopter and an instructor at her disposal.

'There's some French dame coming up here for lessons, just keep her happy – she's a born pilot,' were his terse instructions.

I believe she was the first woman in the United States to get a helicopter licence. Later, when everyone felt she was psychologically equipped for the experience, I arranged for her (still incognito to others) to meet General Vandenberg, on whose staff I served as Advisor to the Women's Air Force – a post to which, coincidentally, I was recommended by the other great lady pilot, Jacqueline Cochran.

Mme Auriol was at last able to get back into a jet, to try out her nerve as well as her skills. Courage won. When she returned to France she went into the air again. But not before a touching experience which nearly destroyed her capacity to go back among people she knew.

FACE

I had taken her out to dine in public for the first time; this, too, would be a test. Would she be ready to see and meet people she knew casually again? I chose a restaurant which I regularly frequented, The Pavilion, because I had a table there and could arrange in advance for a minimum of attention. The two of us were about to slide into the seats of my corner baguette when a visiting French gentleman recognized me. His table was opposite. He stood up, bowed low over my hand, hesitated for a moment after looking at Jacqueline Auriol, then merely smiled and sat down again. No introductions were exchanged.

Mme Auriol knew this much-decorated war hero (he'd lost his leg in the War) far better than I, but he hadn't recognized her, and with her new face, she was far from ready to admit her real identity to someone who ought to have jumped to her side.

Who would have dreamt that we'd find a Frenchman four feet away from us unable to identify her? It was an unfortunate and dramatic situation. The General soon finished his meal and came to the table to say goodbye. Turning from me, he looked intently at my companion – and apologized. Before he turned on his heel and left he said, 'Do forgive me for smiling at you when you came in. For just a fleeting moment, I had the mistaken idea you were Jacqueline Auriol.'

She dissolved in tears; I had to try hard not to do the same.

'I've lost my identity, my own friends don't know me. *Who* am I?' she sobbed.

A NIGHT IN A

Gambling is a national pastime, a routine part of British life – and not only for the rich. The national habit of staking money or any other thing of value on an uncertain outcome has given them the world's record.

Some say gambling was invented by a Chinese Emperor in the twelfth century to amuse his wives, that it was brought to Spain (presumably by gypsies) half a century later. Dostoyevsky's life was nearly ruined by gambling. William Blake wrote that 'the whore and the gambler, the state licensed, build that nation's fate'.

But when gambling was legalized by the Tories in England in the sixties what did they unleash, apart from a sudden emergence of over 1,200 gambling-clubs (and all the new opportunities provided to gangsters)? Two new family diseases were born: mother caught bingo and father got the gambling-club sickness. The illnesses became so prolific, a Gamblers Anonymous was created to deal expressly with the human wrecks – mentally and physically very sick people.

Once contracted, the disease is rarely curable because of the patient's inability to stay away from the source. The worst stage is the final one for those who survive earlier symptoms. It is called compulsive gambling and is developed by a large percentage of players. It is progressive in nature. It can't be cured; with help it can be arrested.

The compulsive gambler must always gamble beyond his means. He loses friends and jobs and destroys his life, with an apparent wish for self destruction. He is in need. He dreams

GAMBLER'S LIFE

about being King for a night. His pleasure is in losing.

Once a person has crossed the invisible line that divides gambling as a simple pastime from irresponsible, uncontrolled gambling, he can never go back.

One such man offers macabre proof in a chilling story, told me by the only woman big-time casino operator in England, a tiny woman from the bogs of Ireland, who ended up the owner of one of London's posh Mayfair clubs.

One of her regular gamblers, a consistent loser, made a sudden killing one night. He found himself with £6,000 ($12,000) in winnings in his hand, his first in years. Somehow he'd kept himself in the game by playing with his wife's house-keeping money, all their savings and with whatever he could realize by selling their household treasures.

The change in his luck was almost too much for him; he rushed home and hysterically woke up his sleeping wife. Flashing the roll of bills at her he shouted: 'It's all yours, it belongs to you, darling! You deserve it. It is yours to spend any way you want.'

Disbelieving, the sad woman sat up in bed staring at the money, disorientated and dazed. Her husband made up her mind: 'We'll take the first plane in the morning to Paris. You're going to go on the spending spree of your life.'

With great thought and care he and his wife tucked the money under the mattress on her side of the bed and exhausted by emotion, both fell asleep.

But the husband couldn't sleep; he suddenly woke up,

terribly anxious. If I am on a winning streak, why do I stop, he kept asking himself. Unable to control his actions, he tip-toed to her side of the bed and with the skill of the depraved silently removed the money under her mattress and fled back to the casino.

'I'll bring her back a real fortune this time – and, believe me, she deserves it,' he assured himself.

He lost every penny. A very dismal man went home and this time fell into a deep stupor. His wife slept through it all, exhausted by emotion and excitement, but woke up at seven –

prepared to take the earliest possible morning plane to Paris. Leaning over, she reached for the money under her mattress. Where was it? Where had it gone? She screamed in distress: 'Where's the money? Where is it? Where is it?'

'What money?' the sleepy man mumbled.

'The £6,000 you won last night,' she cried. 'We put it under the mattress before we went to sleep.'

'You must be mad!' he replied. 'You've been dreaming again and *this time it's a nightmare*! Go back to sleep and leave me alone. *I'm tired.*'

Victor Borge, that superb clown at the piano, once owned a castle just outside Copenhagen called Freydenlund, which had been the summer residence of the last English Queen of Denmark. Among other things, it was renowned for its shape; every important room in the central portion was a circle fifty feet in diameter. Who but Borge would have bought a huge castle with such impossible decorating problems just for the occasional vacation?

But Victor Borge does his best when he isn't being too serious. The home which he bought rather impulsively has since made him, or so it is rumoured, a very large fortune. For one thing, he found a vast deserted apple orchard on its grounds and he turned it into a profit making operation. It always seems to turn out like this for this man with the Midas touch.

He hadn't meant to buy it nor had I meant to persuade him to do so, but on one farcical weekend I managed to do so. The experience is routine to anyone who spends time in his company. Each time can be an exercise fraught with danger for the serious-minded.

Victor Borge, as his enormous audience knows, is either a comedian who plays the piano superbly or a concert pianist who makes topical jokes while doing so. He first played the piano in Copenhagen at the age of three, but his career began at the age of ten when he was hailed as a child prodigy after playing in his first concert, also in Copenhagen. No one realized, least of all Borge, that he was also a funny man. This

VICTOR BORGE

fact came to light after he grew up and was playing in a concert with the Philharmonic in the United States.

The audience first began to snicker at his wildly mis-behaving eyebrow, then broke into laughter – causing the conductor to race his orchestra ahead of the soloist. Borge stopped playing, walked to the conductor's stand, turned the score back several pages, bowed to the orchestra, winked to the audience, returned to his seat, resumed his playing. More roars of laughter.

Suddenly a world-famous comedian had been born. The theatrical one-man show *Comedy in Music* made him a fortune. His humour steadily developed and he never ceased to keep vast audiences laughing on stage and on television.

On 31 July in 1957, Victor Borge went from obscurity in England to being the most talked-of stage personality there. The warm man with the keen wit made theatrical history when he appeared in his one-man performance for a six weeks' season at the Shaftesbury Theatre in London.

Having known him for years, we arranged for him and his wife to spend their weekends with us in our Sussex home. The Benchley wit, the dry style, the insane historical anecdotes, ('by several miles the funniest man in London' as the *Observer* reported) was as funny off-stage as on.

'I love my weekends here,' he announced one day. 'I should buy a country house in Europe, too.'

'But my children are just as much Danish as American,' he announced one Sunday at lunch. 'I should buy a house in

Denmark. I shall bring them there for a few months each year and then they will be really conscious of their Danish origin, they may even learn to speak the language. We must have a place exactly like yours.'

He began to bring me piles of sales brochures on Danish homes, sent by his solicitor from Copenhagen. All were enormous – in fact not at all like the Elizabethan farmhouse we lived in (the inviting scale of which had originally evoked our affection). When a brochure on Freydenlund Castle was offered to me, I burst into laughter. 'That's exactly the place for you!'

He actually bought the castle, and then the madness really started. He insisted that I make good a carelessly made promise to help him 'do up' the place. Not being able to get out of it – and in any case full of curiosity to see his little country weekend house – my husband and I went to Copenhagen a few weeks later for four days. It became an insane buying spree. Antique shops, fabric makers, upholsterers and drapers were dealt with on an assembly-line basis in a surrealistic scramble to buy, buy, buy and to order, order, order.

Before returning to London (having spent Borge's money as if it was just paper) I sat in the centre of the huge empty circular drawing room, making water colour sketches of each room, attaching swatches of fabric, coding and indicating the location of furniture and accessories.

Of course, decorating is not my profession, but I had done many homes of my own in the United States and England, and I thought I knew what Victor Borge wanted. Estimates were demanded and given and okayed, contracts for work given out, delivery schedules arranged – and we left Copenhagen with a promise: the castle would be ready for occupancy the following June. We agreed to fly over again to celebrate the house-warming.

Two months before that, I was awakened in the middle of a cold night by a frantic Victor Borge on the telephone. He'd forgotten the difference in time, and was calling me from Nashville, Tennessee. Terribly distressed, he reported that all my drawings had been lost. 'Can you do another set?' he pleaded. 'No,' I replied. 'It's impossible. You'll have to do something else.'

A few hours later, a cable arrived from him repeating:

'Darling Fleur, Freydenlund colour sketches and swatches lost stop can you re-do them? I'm desperate.'

I had neither the time nor the wish to do it over again. How could I possibly remember the details and colour schemes I'd worked out with such impulsiveness six months before?

But I agreed to try for my old friend. And then the comedy really began. Borge, assuming all would go well the second time round, organized a very special dinner party to in-augurate the castle. The guest list included the American Ambassador to Denmark, Mr Val Peterson and his wife, the Danish Prime Minister, Mr Hansen, and his wife and the Danish Ambassador to the United States and his wife (on holiday in Copenhagen). My husband and I flew from London for the weekend, and Mr and Mrs Borge flew from the United States to meet us there the same day, the Thursday before the party on Saturday.

We were met at the airport by a tearful man, this time more like Chaplin than Borge. Once again the workmen and sup-pliers had let him down. Nothing had been done.

Then began an unbelievable scramble: which of the four Marx Brothers was I supposed to be in this farce, I kept asking myself. There were only two days to furnish an empty castle before the dinner.

My husband remembers his contribution with glee, having to do something most men and women have longed to do – driving Borge's huge American station wagon from florist to florist, he swept up and bought the entire contents of every shop! 'I'll take everything!' he'd say to their astonishment. Flowers, we had decided, would compensate for missing furniture in the circular room. Oliver Messel would have approved.

Hundreds of yards of sheeting was bought and windows were swagged in rich triple folds, filled in by huge buckets of flowers, banked by massed potted plants. Furniture (just enough to seat the exact number of guests) was borrowed from an antique shop to enable us to sit in the drawing room for the routine short period of polite conversation before and after dinner, which was to begin at six o'clock and end at a very early hour.

A good staff, including a fine cook, was somehow organ-ized. A dining room was created out of paperhanger's tables, a huge one for dining, and two smaller ones for serving tables.

More sheeting replaced the linen we didn't have – draped and tacked to the wooden bases, seams disguised by garlands of flowers. No setting could be prettier or more precarious.

When, at ten minutes to six, the front door bell rang, hearts sank. We were losing ten golden minutes. Prime Minister Hansen and his wife had arrived early.

My husband and Borge's wife greeted the distinguished pair at the door, trying to preserve precious minutes by prolonging the welcome in the front hall. Borge and I hastily finished the dining room, raced up the back stairs, changed clothes like lightning and dashed down the front steps, breathless but apologetic.

There was one final memorable note: the Prime Minister's wife tightly clutched a stiff bouquet of orange carnations wrapped in silver foil. Nothing was left to put them in – nothing – nor did I want the colour to clash in the drawing room which I'd kept to pinks and reds and blues. How would Groucho Marx have dealt with this bouquet, I asked myself? I whispered to Victor's wife Anna to explain they would be so nice on her bedside table and they were quickly whisked away.

The one thing missing from one of the merriest dinner parties in history was a recorder to tape the hilarious conversation. Borge, in top form, brought the best out of everyone. We were weary from laughter, forgetting our desperate fatigue, when we said farewell to the last guest.

Months later, the furniture and accessories finally did arrive at the castle, and the Borges enjoyed their 'folly' to the full. However, not for long. Freydenlund was soon sold for an undisclosed large profit.

PERUVIAN

For years I have been obsessed by the longing for two seemingly unobtainable paintings in Peru. Their beauty was compelling: voluptuous frames surrounding works of art – very small paintings encased in frames immensely larger than they, made of rich square mirrors inset in tiny pieces of gold, intricately patterned to catch the sun or reflect the evening's light. Despite the disparity in size between paintings and frames, each subject had a compelling intensity.

I always wanted to have them but it took ten years for me to own them. I had abandoned all thought of getting them and, in any case, a project of enormous scale took precedence over all others when I purchased the ruins of an ancient castle-fortress in Spain's remote Extramadura. I embarked on years of work in restoring it to its original statuesque beauty – and forgot all about paintings from Peru.

The Extramadura is the Spanish province which produced all the Conquistadores, those men who left Spain and discovered, captured and destroyed so much of Mexico and Peru. From my town, Trujillo, above which my castle sits, nineteen important men went abroad to become a part of history.

The ancestors of Pissaro, who was born in a house close by, and possibly also of Cortes who came from a nearby village, have been reported in local accounts to have lived in this fortress-castle.

The countryside, which I love and see so clearly from my windows, has panoramic vistas. Perhaps it was this harsh

PORTRAIT

outlook as much as the extreme poverty of the land which drove men from the area to seek their fortunes elsewhere, to take their chances in mysterious new lands, crossing the Atlantic in tiny vessels to do so.

Cortes led his men to Mexico. Pissaro landed in Peru. Their victories were accomplished by devastating heroism coupled with barbaric massacres and total destruction of the people and civilizations they found there. Pissaro, their perversely heroic leader, found an elegant empire in Peru, but killed and looted as he went, and contributed little or nothing in exchange. A religious fervour had helped them keep going, but their real lust was for gold, and all among them enjoyed fighting to get it.

The arid Extramadura world they left behind is little changed today. I have contributed my small bit by restoring the ancient castle with love and care, retaining all I could of the beauties left behind by the Romans, the Visigoths, the Moors and, finally, the Spaniards, who reclaimed it from the Arabs. All around me I see the same unyielding land they knew; scrub oak is still the only green foliage and it still provides the fodder as it did then for the pigs from which now come the famed *Jamon Montanchez*. The one crop is wheat and this can usually only be grown every two years.

In many places, the drama comes from a Martian landscape, stunning to look at but impossible to live on, land dominated by bare rock crops as high as twelve feet above the ground.

Not many steps outside my walls high up on our hill, is the

Church of Santa Marta, which looks down on exactly the same stone buildings Pissaro would have seen in his childhood in the early sixteenth century. Many of these were built as homes for the Court of Queen Isabella, who chose to have a vast summer palace here after the Moors were dispersed. And no wonder: the Moors had left behind vestiges of hundreds of years of productive sovereignty, an elegant culture and a generally benign and generous rule.

Peru is now seldom mentioned there, but it is still a part of the bones and body of Extramadura. Sadly, there is no sign (not *one*) of the gold which ancestors fought so hard to bring back. It is said that Napoleon, defeated by Wellington on the plains below, had commanded his men to ransack and loot Trujillo as they fled through it in retreat, a bedraggled army taking the loot in lieu of any other payment. Every church, every castle, every public building was stripped of all golden artifacts which were probably all melted down.

When restoring my castle, I felt I must endow it with a monastic simplicity and this I did with basic white walls sparsely punctuated by antiques. I designed most of the furniture in stone, made by local stone-masons using the skills handed down from the Romans. All is prim and neat, made gay by accessories.

Outside, above high walls, I see only other crenellations. In order to reach the gate-house, one must climb up the same narrow, winding road built by the Romans alongside a Hamlet backdrop. Once inside my gates, there is a green Moorish garden, astounding in the dry land – an oasis watered from an enormous Moorish cistern unexpectedly found underground. There is always the sound the Moors loved and understood so well, that of running water, to refresh the air and the mind.

With this as a mental picture, may I take you back to the saga of the two paintings in Peru: they now hang in Conquistadores country, on the walls of our sixty-five foot living room, completely at home in their environment (obviously they'd look very strange elsewhere) between two beautiful fifteen feet wide doors. One is a portrait head of a splendidly handsome gentleman, seven inches by ten inches, surrounded by the gold and mirror frame which narrows down from three feet wide by five feet deep at the outer edge to the tiny size of the portrait itself. The frame slopes twenty-one inches from portrait to wall.

The other is also a very small painting, a conversation piece of a family enjoying their garden (in Peru?) This frame is equally large but only thirteen inches deep, baroque at its best.

Their arrival in Trujillo was accomplished by intrigue and good luck. A devoted friend of mine became Ambassador to the Argentine four years before. He also had the peripheral countries of Paraguay, Uruguay, Chile, Colombia, Bolivia and Peru in which to represent his country. He gallantly persisted in trying to locate them for me and he finally succeeded.

The castle in Spain had just been furnished when (quite without knowing this fact) the Ambassador sent me a cable asking where to ship them. To Trujillo, of course – *a bit of Peru.*

The real significance of their being in Trujillo didn't surface until a New Year's Day luncheon party there for many of my Extramadura and Madrid friends. When they spotted the portrait of the elegant gentleman there was excitement.

'Do you know *who* he is?' they wanted to know. I didn't.

The aquiline face, looking very regal, *was* in fact very regal. It was of Inca Garcelaso de la Vega (a name, we have since discovered, is painted almost imperceptibly and almost out of sight, near the portrait's frame).

The Prince was the son of Princess Isabel Chimpu Occlo – niece of one of the last of the great Inca rulers, Nuayna Capac – hence his royal title. His father, Captain Sebastian Garcelaso de la Vega, a victorious Conquistador who had left Trujillo, lived in Cuzco after his marriage, governed it from 1553 until his death in 1559. The young Prince then left for Spain to see the land of his father, and never returned to Peru. It is said he came to live in Trujillo, as his father had done.

The impact made on him of the fourteen years he spent with his mother's people before he left Peru is shown in a remarkable book, *Royal Commentaries of the Incas* which was published in Spain forty-eight years after his arrival and is now considered by some as a literary masterpiece. The contents were then, and still are, referred to as an undeniable history of Peru's conquest by the Spaniards. In Peru at least, his name is lauded as the great writer of their glorious past. He died in

1616 – oddly enough the same year as Cervantes and Shakespeare.

As recently as 1978, King Juan Carlos of Spain, while on a state visit to Peru, returned to the people of Cuzco, the ancient Imperial city of the Incas, the urn containing Garcelaso de la Vega's ashes, from the vault in Cordoba where he was buried.

My obsession brought the Inca's portrait back to the land of the Conquistadores which he had learned to love. If he could speak, what would he say?

I don't know how Ruskin would now describe the jet age we live in but he once wrote morbidly that railroad travel 'transmits a man into a living parcel'. He would surely recognize us as human missiles as we now hurtle through the air in a Concorde.

Trains evoke other definitions to other people, especially those who tend to glamorize the deluxe long-distance runs. To millions of other commuters, the train is a humdrum necessity of daily life as they shuttle back and forth to work.

A few still dream. To them, the word train conjures up danger, misery, romance – even the macabre. *Danger* is a James Bond stealing steadily along the corridors of the Orient Express; *misery* is the man, woman and child jammed like animals into box-cars destined for concentration camps and extermination; *romance* is a Marlene Dietrich waiting, huddled, in the corner of a private compartment.

To my husband, during the last War, a train became a macabre tableau, witnessed in a dark and dirty box-car as a prisoner of war. He'd been in an officers' prison camp in Czechoslovakia, having been moved from camp to camp until he'd been in most of them in all Nazi-held countries. Somehow, the German military had just learned that he and other prisoners were in communication with the local Czech underground so it was decided to move the camp quickly, and somewhat harshly, to the heart of Germany. Twenty prisoners, each deprived of their shoes and braces, were put in handcuffs and allotted half a freight-car. Across the centre dividing the car, was a barbed wire fence. Like cattle, they travelled to a new destination, just as unpleasant as the one left behind.

Behind the barbed wire, in the other half of the train, a table was placed – on it a machine-gun, with stick hand-grenades alongside. Six German soldiers sat there with their rifles at the ready, for five long days and nights.

On the fourth night, just as dawn appeared, my husband found himself the only prisoner awake on his side of the wire. In the quiet greyness, he watched a young, smooth-faced German (an Iron-crossed survivor of the Russian front) on the other side. He had placed an incongruous object next to his machine gun, a *small circular hand mirror.*

By the light of the dawn entering through a slatted window behind the man, my husband watched the German sitting there, applying make-up, caressing his face, quite unaware of the silent observer on the other side of the barbed wire.

Other less grim journeys involve romance. In 1900, an English businessman, an associate of my husband's late father, went to the United States, taking Horace Greeley's advice to young men to go west. San Francisco was his destination after boarding a train at New York City.

In those days, trains travelled on single tracks, only branching out onto two tracks to disgorge and pick up passengers at stations or to stop at sidings at regular intervals on long stretches of the road to allow another train going in the opposite direction to slip past.

The young man on the west–bound train, quietly minding his business, sat in his chair with a head full of dreams about the exciting world ahead. The journey was almost half over when suddenly the train slowed down to pull into a station; at the same time, a train destined for New York pulled along-side. Casually staring through his window, he blinked hard. Could the beautiful girl sitting two panes away from him in the seat alongside in the other train actually be real? He'd never seen anyone lovelier.

In the fleeting minutes it took him to leap from one train to the other, he knew this was the girl he wanted to marry. Undaunted, he slipped into the seat alongside her and he promptly proposed. Two strangers looked at each other with amazement and wonder. As the train moved away from the station toward New York, they realized it was love at first sight. She accepted his proposal, and they were married at journey's end, moving soon to England, all thoughts of an American career now put aside. The son of this remarkable pair is now a prominent banker, who was at his parents' side as they celebrated their Golden Anniversary in London.

Not every romantic journey ends so perfectly. To one man, it was ruinous – and provides the main story; about a routine journey regularly made by a Londoner to and from Scotland, which led to disaster. The man in his mid–thirties hadn't the slightest premonition of disaster when he started out on one such once–a–month visit to an aged Scottish uncle. As sole heir to both his title and fortune, the nephew was most attentive to the very old man.

When the attractive gentleman arrived on the platform at the London railway station, he was surprised to find that the sleeper train was late in arriving, so he joined the others strolling up and down the platform. One of them was a handsome girl who seemed his own age so he quite naturally started up a conversation. When the train arrived, they were pleased to discover they had both been allotted sleeping berths in the same car.

She accepted his invitation to have a nightcap from the bottle of whisky he always carried in his bag. After five drinks, it seemed pointless for her to return to her own berth. The next morning, he was startled and dismayed to discover that she was not only the secret new wife of his elderly uncle but also his hostess for the weekend.

He was much more surprised, nine months later, when she gave birth to a son. That baby became the new heir to his uncle's title and vast fortune, displacing him completely.

Another train tale is a war tale which happened one night in the third year of the last War when 1,500 allied prisoners, all officers including my husband, were forced into cattle trucks in Northern Italy by bad-tempered German troops. It was a long train with every five box cars punctuated by a flat car on which the Germans mounted heavy machine-guns – determined that none should escape. Naturally, their destination was unknown but all knew it would be northward from Bologna and over the mountains into Germany.

First inspection by the cramped men revealed they were in old and rotting cattle trucks. Soon after they began to move, they hacked away at the boarded walls of their moving prison, using implements that ranged from forks or knives to the more efficient pieces of heavier metal they had accumulated and hidden over months, even years.

The journey, which progressed at a snail's pace, was one of constant stops and starts – the rumble of wheels over poor tracks and the drawn-out screeching of brakes at interminable halts. Prisoner of war trains were a low priority on the rails which were used for troop reinforcements, for ammunition and fuel – which roared past them at an envied clip.

After two days and two nights, the foothills of the Alps were finally reached. The knowledgeable among them, peering through their newly made slits, thought the Pass they would be using was the Brenner. There had been many attempts at escape en-route, most of them crude, ('just jump and run and hope') followed by a burst of machine-gun fire, much shouting and either injury or death for the escapee – always recapture.

The central character of this story was a noted British actor who'd been captured in the African desert in the early days of the War and was smarting under several years of internment in Italian prisoner of war camps. He didn't relish the idea of being in even worse German hands. He had spent the last day and night on the train quietly thinking and watching. At last his chosen opportunity arrived as the train ground to another halt at the tiny one-sided apology for a station. In a garage, covered in pine alongside was a halted string of box cars carrying ammunition, unguarded.

He and his friends had rendered two planks weak by constant attacks with their knives (no ordinary ones, these – sharp edges had been altered to resemble miniature swords after formidable and painstaking work). Kicking away the two planks he gently slid through the hole into the darkness below. Night was falling and his cover was aided by the shadows cast by the train alongside. After previous stops, he knew exactly how station guards would look and he had done his best to become one of them. In his rough–hewn clothes he actually resembled the scruffy rail-workers in their indifferent shabby outfits, and their sameness was accentuated by his two days' growth of beard.

He felt the lovely touch of gravel beneath his feet and this gave him encouragement. Drawing upon the confidence gained after years on the stage, he strode toward the rear of the train and mounted the wooden staging which passed for a station platform, playing his part with casual perfection. From his left-hand pocket, he took out the handkerchief which had taken so long to tint a shade of green (using the juices of that rarity, a vegetable).

From his right-hand pocket he took out a whistle, gained in a hassle with an unsuspecting guard.

With splendid gusto, he blew hard and long on his whistle, waving the green go-ahead handkerchief with conventional irritation. The driver of the train, just discernible in the distance, replied with the customary toot of his whistle. Slowly the train inched forward to the Brenner Pass, carrying guards, Germans, machine-guns.

Suddenly, all was quiet, nothing moving. With an eerie feeling, he realized he was all alone, a solitary figure on a tiny enemy platform. He was free.

THE FUNERAL

The former President of the United States, Harry S. Truman, went as the personal representative of President Lyndon B. Johnson to the funeral of King Paul of Greece. As a friend of the Royal family, I went from London.

The funeral was exhausting. Like so many orthodox church services, the ritualistic Greek Orthodox Mass began at a very early hour, requiring everyone to rise and to breakfast at an unaccustomed time. The ceremony was full of pageantry and sadness for those who loved him, as I did.

Though in a Mediterranean city, the day was raw, the church frigid and we had to sit out the drama and beauty of the very long service on very hard seats. After the ceremony, the mourners gathered outside and formed into a massive parade, to march through Athens behind the coffin. The church is at the lowest point of the city, making the march through Athens an arduous one – all uphill – until the brow of the hill was reached just outside the Hilton Hotel, overlooking the sprawling city below.

The coffin made its way on the shoulders of a guard of honour. At the junction where mourners gathered again, the body was placed on any army catafalque to make its slow journey thirty miles outside Athens to the private Royal home, called *Tatoi*, outside the city.

I'd grown to know this lovely house after years of visits there; *Tatoi* was a highly personal, rambling, chintz-filled, bookish house, with a fascinating collection of ancient *objets*. This country home was the family's real home; the Royal

OF A KING

Palace in Athens, vast and impersonal, was used for office and ceremonies.

The following day, I went to the Hilton Hotel to pay my respects to Mr Truman, whom I'd known since he became President. He was by then an old man and should have been very weary. He absolutely denied it.

'I was worried about you yesterday, but I couldn't find you. How did you survive that strenuous, tiring walk? You must have been exhausted,' I said. (It had intrigued me, by the way, that the Archbishop, over eighty and much more frail than Mr Truman, had made the trip on foot, leading the procession holding a heavy ancient icon above his head all the while.)

Mr Truman's face came alive in consternation. 'Who was tired? I wasn't. Why should I be? – I didn't walk a step. I sat in a big comfortable limousine, following the parade!'

I was delighted to hear the good news, pleased though not surprised that arrangements had been made to ease the trip for him.

Next, I wondered about food. How had he managed to wait for the late luncheon (nearly four o'clock) after such an early breakfast?

'Who starved?' he replied with a wide grin and a glint in his eyes. 'If you'd seen me in the car, you'd know I had brought my own chicken sandwiches.'

I constantly enjoy that image of one of the greatest American Presidents, a little man sunk at the back of a huge black car on a state occasion, munching away at a brown paper bag full of food.

ELSA'S

I normally go from London to the United States twice yearly. When the lady-giants of the seas, the *Queens*, were sailing, I often sailed on the way out, to arrive rested enough to cope with the hectic period ahead. The trips were usually professional ones – either to launch a new book or open an exhibition of my paintings.

On one such journey, I received a cable on the *Queen Mary* from a friend who was a famous animal conservationist – asking if I'd dine with him and his wife on the night of arrival. I cabled a ready acceptance, grateful for the thoughtfulness and looking forward to a small, pleasurable evening.

The ship was late docking after a particularly rough passage. There were porter-problems as well but I finally reached the St Regis Hotel – weary but elated where I found a warm note of welcome from my hosts, enclosing the guest list for the dinner (and the extraordinary location).

It was pages long. After finally counting up the numbers, the thought of dining with three hundred others in a restaurant on top of the skyscraper called Rockefeller Center was a terrifying one. My fears were not allayed when I stood in the receiving line later, to meet one of New York City's liveliest crowds, many of them complete strangers.

We were finally directed to tables of ten and I felt better. It was easy to adopt the pretence that there were only these few for dinner, simply by ignoring the other tables and concentrating on mine. Suddenly, however, I discovered the peculiar configuration of the huge round Rainbow Room, fifty storeys above the city.

LION

The room was marked out into three movable circular areas, each inside the other – the smallest in the centre, with the largest one outside the rim of the intermediate size. As I sat in my chair in the centre circle, I realized that each of the other two circles were revolving slowly, very slowly, around us – in almost imperceptible movement.

This meant that what you saw (if you looked between the guests at other tables) kept changing – new faces constantly appeared. In fact, whole new tables came into view as they inched around on their quiet machinery. I pitied the waiters.

It was a surrealist evening, ensured by the presence of that master surrealist, Salvador Dali, dressed in his usual unconventional garb, his long upturned moustaches twitching as he spoke in his somewhat halting English (interspersed with Catalan).

I was on my host's right and, on his left, was the late Mrs Joy Adamson of *Born Free* and Elsa the Lion fame. The famous animal lover never even noticed Dali, so absorbed was she in pinning down the host with her message on conservation. On my right was Salvador Dali.

As I've written the authorized biography, *The Case of Salvador Dali* and we were old friends, we were also absorbed in talk – until a guest at the other side of the round table leaned over and asked, loud enough to be heard over the din, when my exhibition would be opening. As I so often paint the jungle cats and foliage, birds and flowers, someone else asked if I'd done any cheetahs.

The word brought Mrs Adamson to sudden attention.

Ignoring what we were saying, she launched into a quick bitter speech on saving the cheetah from extinction. There wouldn't be another cheetah left in future if something wasn't done at once to save them. The messianic glint in her eye provoked our host to suggest that she ask Salvador Dali about disappearing wild life.

'Salvador Dali! He's here?' demanded the lady.

'Of course, he's next to Fleur Cowles,' he explained.

From that moment on, no one else even existed; all her attention was riveted on Dali. 'You paint animals,' she announced to him. 'You must make me a painting to be used as a poster for my campaign to save the big cats!'

She may have decided to talk to Dali but he had no wish to reply. He had been talking to me when interrupted by her (without his permission). 'Tell her,' he said, caustically refusing to look at her and only speaking directly to me, 'that I don't paint animals.'

'He doesn't paint animals,' I repeated, turning left to her across my host.

'Yes he does! I know his work,' she announced.

'Yes you do, she says,' I repeated, turning to Mr Dali.

'Tell her I don't,' he insisted.

'He insists he doesn't,' I repeated to her.

There I was, dead-centre of a tennis match – a referee having to turn left to listen to one and then promptly turning to my right to repeat what she had said. Back and forth and back and forth I went for the next ten hilarious minutes; all other conversation stopped dead amid peals of laughter.

'Yes, you *must* give me a painting,' she persisted firmly. I repeated this to Dali, who still refused to look at her.

LION

'Please tell her I don't *give*,' he replied, emphasizing this most vital point with a sharp quiver of his moustache.

'He doesn't *give*,' I turned to her to repeat, trying to reproduce his icy tone to the lady.

'He *must* give. He loves animals and *must* support their cause.'

I turned to Dali to repeat the riposte.

'I hate animals,' Dali replied. 'Tell her.'

'He hates animals,' I repeated.

'He can't hate animals. He paints them so well.'

'You can't hate them and paint them so well, Dali, she insists!'

'Tell her I know what I hate. I hate animals. I no paint animals. I *kill!*'

'Mr Dali,' I echoed dutifully, 'hates animals. He doesn't paint them. He kills them. . .'

'Impossible!'

'She says it's impossible.'

The by now crazy game might have dragged on endlessly until Dali struck the *coup de grace.*

'Tell the lady I have one lion. I kill him.'

'No!!'

I told him 'No!'

'Yes I do! Tell lady I put lion in cage – solid gold cage. I give lion Salvador Dali diet – emeralds, rubies, sapphires – nothing else!'

'But lions don't eat stones!' she sneered.

'She says (and she ought to know),' I repeated, 'that lions don't eat stones.'

'Aha! That is right,' Dali smugly replied. 'Lion no like jewellery. Lion die. Me *happy*.'

THE AIR AGE

Coming back from a trip I made to Brazil (I'd gone for President Eisenhower, to see Osvaldo Aranha and President Vargas), I found Maurice Schumann, France's Foreign Secretary, on my plane. We talked incessantly of the state of Brazil in the fifties, of the wealth under its soil, of its physical beauty, its size, the condition of millions of poor – comparing stories. Was it or wasn't it the country with its future behind it (as everyone still asks)?

As we neared New York, Mr Schumann turned to me with a smile and said, 'I will give you the best story of all. Take it as a gift and tell it when you want to describe Brazil dramatically. It deserves re-telling, but I'll be too pre-occupied when I get to France.'

Time hasn't lessened its interest – for me, it still is a dramatic way to describe, timelessly, the Brazil of the end of the last War, with colossal unpopulated areas, illiterate populations, and little productive capacity – not exactly like the Brazil of today, a hubbub of activity over and under its rich, rich soil and its exploding population (over 100,000,000 people, half of them under eighteen)! Their economic problems kept multiplying.

The story had first been told to the Foreign Minister of France before he told it to me on that plane ride. He'd been assured it had actually happened to a princely heir of the last King of Brazil, whose one consuming passion was aviation. A friend of the Prince had returned from the interior on a hunting trip near the Amazon.

IN BRAZIL

Immediately on arrival he had gone to the Prince to plead with him to fly to a village he'd just been through so that he could rescue a dying boy of eight or nine.

The prince heard the story and agreed to help. He took off on the rescue mission in his small single-engined plane, fortified by a detailed navigational drawing made by his friend to indicate where to set down in a clearing near the boy's village. His father, the village's Indian Chief, would be there to welcome him. All had been pre-arranged by the original traveller.

When the plane landed, it in itself caused little stir. The visit of a genuine member of the Royal Family was much more exciting. The Indians had become used to planes flying overhead and took the arrival of one on the ground as nearly normal. After formal greetings were over, the Prince asked to see the sick child he'd come to rescue. He soon realized how ill the boy was, and that he was almost totally paralysed.

'Could I take the boy to be treated in a big city nearby?' he asked.

Only because he was descended from a great king was such a suggestion received without anger and threats. The idea of a hospital was both strange and unacceptable to Indians whose fate was always in the hands of their Medicine Man. Still, the special visitor couldn't be insulted and an agreement was slowly and reluctantly given.

The Prince carefully picked up the little boy and carried him in his own arms to the plane. The entire village hovered in awe and concern as he gently placed him on the floor. Faces grew grim as he closed the door and prepared to take off in haste before suspicions could break out in dangerous ways. He gathered altitude as fast as the plane allowed, leaving behind a small group of uncertain, uncivilized Indians in a trail of dust on the clearing.

Flying towards Sao Paulo, he was fascinated by the child; he hadn't made a sound or a whimper, though his bright feverish eyes never left the Prince's face. He simply stared, without expression, through the journey, somehow indicating he was still alive, though never moving even an inch. A trust developed as they flew to their destination.

The airport at Sao Paulo had been alerted. So had the hospital – and an ambulance waited at the end of the runway for the private plane. The Prince brought his machine down as gently as possible, not to frighten the boy or to cause him pain. He jumped out quickly and dashed round to the other side to assure the boy all was well. When he opened the door the boy could see outside. He turned deathly pale and in a burst of fear suddenly began to scream hysterically.

What caused this terror? The Prince later explained – and it is the entire point of the story: the boy had grown up accustomed to seeing the monstrous birds flying through the skies above him, but when he saw motor cars and vans darting busily like bees across the airport on the ground level, he was chilled with horror. He knew flying birds but he had never seen a *wheel*!

'Brazil has been born in the *air* age. It *should* move ahead fast,' was the French Foreign Minister's closing comment.

A WOMAN

A frail distinguished lady, suffering from a bad back, sat in the cold for two and a half hours on a grey, rainy day – waiting for a Parade to begin. She was in a grandstand outside Lancaster House facing the processional route of Coronation participants and special guests. The location was considered a special one but it cannot have pleased the woman, who expected to be in Westminster Abbey itself.

It was in June, 1953, when young Queen Elizabeth II was about to be crowned. I attended the event as an American Ambassador. So also did Earl Warren, then Governor of California and later to be the Chief Justice of the United States, and General Owen Bradley, who represented the Armed Forces. Also, that most adored of all Americans in England that day, General George Catlett Marshall, who came as President Eisenhower's personal delegate.

The day had begun at an extremely early hour for the woman sitting in the stand. At eight o'clock (a long time before our delegation was needed) she had taken her place, having risen much earlier than we. Our delegation, as I will explain later, was given special dispensation – more time to wake from the torpor of pleasant fatigue before beginning our long, long day. Our longest day, in fact.

We had been fully briefed and were ready for it. Each morning of the celebrations (at an hour which sometimes seemed like dawn) our exhausted group were given enormous charts, twice as wide as deep, covered with enough detail to do justice to an army landing.

IN A TAXI

The British are rightly famed for their meticulous detail in connection with royal occasions and had responded with remarkable skill to the challenge of what had been considered the last great royal occasion the world would see (not prophesying the marriage of Prince Charles and Lady Diana). Those in charge of events had worked out, in minute detail, just what would be the strategic points of each day's events; we knew from our 'operational charts' exactly what time we were obliged to leave the hotel (and we never left a moment later), when and where we'd eat, when to go to (and/or leave) a party, when expected at the next port of call, when and if a change of clothes was required (and if so *exactly* what to wear) – down to jewellery (such information was supplied to me in advance before leaving home), who of any family which might also have come to London was invited to a given event (or whether spouses or children were meant to go off and sight-see; even this was pre-arranged) and how much time they had to do it in.

The logistics on Coronation Day itself were the most astonishing – especially the fitting of each car of each delegation into the Coronation procession. As an American, I was extremely fortunate; because of General Marshall's age and his position, it was arranged that he and I, in one car, should be the car next to the last in the long procession of other such guests as Maharajahs, sultans, commonwealth prime ministers. Princes and princesses of royal blood – and, of course, the Royal Family itself came after us in the line-up.

This gave us a slightly longer night's rest followed by the shortest possible wait in the church, and we were grateful: others had to begin to arrive at six in the morning; we arrived just after nine.

Everything had been rehearsed by the Coronation officials beforehand, down to split seconds. We knew what time a staff officer would awaken us, when breakfast would be at the door, when the lifts set aside for our exclusive use would be open and waiting for us. We even knew who went first into our motor car, to avoid losing a moment in unnecessary *politesse*.

We left for Westminster Abbey exactly at the moment expected. The speed at which our car would drive between the hotel and the Coronation procession had been rehearsed and fixed so that we actually entered the Coronation procession without changing our pace, or expecting anyone else to do so to let us in. We simply glided from our street into an empty space which had been maintained in the parade for us.

Meanwhile, the elderly woman sat despondently in the cold on what Art Buchwald called 'England's wettest hour'. As a gesture to her, the Commander in Chief of the Royal Marines, General Sir Leslie Hollis, had offered to be her escort, almost heartbroken about it but gallant enough to give up his treasured place in the Abbey to do so. They arrived at their places when it was still somewhat dark, by taxi.

At 10.00 a.m., she began to feel utterly miserable; her back acted up and she must privately have been somewhat out of sorts for not having been given a seat inside the Abbey. She was only one of many thousands who felt they too deserved the same good fortune, but the old Abbey stone was filled to capacity without them.

Wouldn't she like to wait inside Lancaster House? The

General kept asking. No, she insisted on waiting outside to see the Queen go by, and at 10.45 they were finally able to do so.

When asked then what she'd like to do, she looked the man directly in the face and said, 'General, I want to go home.' This was at least two hours before others could do so.

Home meant the hotel at the end of the Coronation route which, quite naturally, was entirely shut to traffic. Such guests on such special grandstands were, in fact, in an area sealed-off from the rest of London by nine-foot high barricades.

General Hollis knew he had no choice but to get her home – but how? Fortunately, the Lord Chamberlain's officials were in Lancaster House and that helped. With tremendous difficulty a taxi was actually produced. All that was left for General Hollis was to get it and themselves down the Coronation route (there was no other way to go) *in reverse direction*!

The first of many obstacles was the Royal Engineer's Band waiting at the bottom of St James's Street. The General had the problem of persuading the commanding officer to move his band to let their taxi through to the route stretching before them. The road was totally empty; the usually busy traffic lane was packed on all sides but deserted down the middle. Thousands of men and women stood alongside. Suddenly, the crowds saw a sight they couldn't believe: a black taxi was scuttling down the Mall – a taxi going at the fastest possible clip – in the 'wrong' direction.

That is, *between* hurdles. There were still three bands and two lots of troops to manoeuvre out of the way until, finally, 'Wrong-Way Taxi' reached the hotel. It was a trip a certain taxi driver will never forget.

Nor will the woman who was in the taxi, Mrs George C. Marshall, wife of the distinguished General.

Eccentrics abound in England, where they are highly prized; but not all live there. Entirely by accident, I once found quite a lovable one in Denmark.

My husband and I had been motoring, the car radio turned on. Suddenly we were listening to dogs barking out the 'Oh Susannah' song in perfect tune and rhythm. I telephoned the BBC for information. We had been listening, they explained, to an American hit parade record. The dogs were Danish. Their 'conductor' lived in Copenhagen.

This was too amusing a situation to ignore. We had time, in those days, for impulsive journeys – so we flew to Copenhagen for the weekend to locate the man and his musical animals. I went to the editor of the city's top newspaper and introduced myself. Fortunately, he knew my name, connecting it with the publishing world I'd just left, and designated a lovely English-speaking girl reporter to help us find the man.

His name was Carl Wiseman, and he was exactly the sort of nature-lover whom you'd expect would be captivated by all animal sounds. Though shy and modest, he was perfectly willing to discuss his technique. My mental image of dogs lined up in a neat row to bark on command (and in tune) was promptly dispelled. No, there never was a magically-trained pack of dogs with differing barks, responding instantly to a man's baton. What seemed impossible was impossible.

Instead, Mr Wiseman explained, 'You take five dogs. You make a couple of grimaces. You make the dogs bark. You let your tape-recorder run. You then cut the tapes in exactly the

AND THREE TREES

COPYRIGHT *NEW YORKER*

right places and glue the pieces together again. You make music to accompany it. . .And then you wait for someone to be interested in what you've done.'

Wiseman was still hunting for new dog sounds when we met. He boasted happily that he'd managed to get some handsome basses and a few beautiful baritones from St Bernards, a perfect Rottweiter-tenor from some Alsatians and a couple of sopranos from a poodle.

'There is a science to taping a dog's barks,' he explained. 'They are worthless unless the barks are loud and clear. It is useless to tape a bark when a dog is in an attacking position. When it calms down, you get the single, powerful "Wow" you need. Only then do I press the button.'

Wiseman had problems preventing dogs from getting soppy. They all liked him, wagged their tails, rubbed against his legs and whimpered sweet little noises. 'Only when I put on a strict face and make ugly signs do they react properly. And they have to be under three years of age, which is when the voices are finest.'

He later took us to the Zoo, to watch him collect sounds of growling bears, roaring lions and baying hyenas – all for radio and television. He was known in that world as the 'poor millionaire' because his income, royalties from a hit-parade record, was only on paper. He was certainly still poor, with very few pennies in his pockets, but he knew he'd soon be wealthy.

'What are you going to do with all your money when you finally do collect it?' I asked.

'Birds are my real interest. I shall use my money for a very special mission. . .I shall bring honour to my king and my country with the profound ornithological findings on birds I intend to announce to the world.'

'Is it a secret?' I enquired, or could he tell us about this important mission?

He was all too anxious to talk to someone about his Grand Plan: the money, he explained, would buy the finest sound equipment available in the world and be built into a lavish caravan – 'just like the big ones the television people use here. But this one is going to New Zealand.'

'Why New Zealand?' I asked.

Although he also intended to get to the Celebes Island in

AND THREE TREES

Indonesia (where his brother had worked before being shot by the Japanese during the Second World War), it was on getting first to New Zealand that he had set his heart. There he could 'honour his king and country' by revealing a startling discovery about certain birds.

'But why New Zealand?' I insisted.

It was just as easy to pry that answer from him: 'I'm going to visit an old friend, who emigrated there many years before from England. He, too, loved birds so much that he carried out thirty-four species of English songbirds with him to keep England "alive" for him with English sounds!'

'Descendants of twenty-six of those thirty-four varieties are still alive there now,' Wiseman explained. 'I will solve the unanswered question about those which remain – for all other ornithologists elsewhere: *did those English birds learn to sing with a New Zealand accent or had the birds of New Zealand acquired an English accent?*

'It is my dream in life to prove to the world which it is before I die,' he explained as we drifted away to return to our own world.

Another nature story is about a man and three trees. He was past middle-age and was deeply admired by his colleagues. He had left academic life to join the largest timber company in British Colombia. He was accepted as the greatest expert on the forests of that western province.

Though less agile than in his youth, he still loved to leave his office behind and venture forth amid the trees whenever possible, with a young assistant carrying the heavier camping and cooking equipment needed for forays into the depths of the forests.

In the summer's warmth, like a true woodsman, he liked to visit one of his favourite haunts – a truly remote area where virgin trees had been undisturbed for hundreds of years – rarely if ever visited by man. He, alone, had made this area his own personal territory.

On one such trip, it was mid-afternoon when with his assistant he rounded the top corner of a little lake to come to the place he loved most. There grew three perfect specimens of virgin Douglas Fir, each one over ten feet in diameter and two hundred feet in height. Their dark evergreen branches only began to spread one hundred feet above the ground, forming giant umbrellas in the sky. Under their majestic shade he always felt a deep contentment.

This time a terrible sight awaited him: the centre tree was no longer there. It had somehow turned into a vast pile of fresh timber slivers, none over twelve inches in length. Even more uncomfortable and eerie was the fact that the slivers were piled neatly into a huge cone, two hundred feet in diameter and seventy to eighty feet at its highest point. The chips were all new, bright and shining in the afternoon sun.

He was fascinated, then totally amazed. Never in the whole of his career had he heard of or seen anything like this mysterious phenomenon. His assistant was aghast, speechless.

AND THREE TREES

He walked around the pile many times. He picked up and handled the chips. His mind raced. He looked for burn marks, for signs of an explosion – for any clue. What could have caused this precisely arranged disintegration of two hundred tons of standing tree? The chips were fresh; it could only have happened recently. The two men, in fact, were a three-day journey from the nearest human habitation – so what unseen force had been there before them?

At the end of an hour, he stopped examining the evidence. He looked up at the two tall remaining companions still standing, their branches gently stirred by a light breeze giving a comforting rustling sound.

Suddenly, he realized that even he, the forest expert, would never know what occurred. He would never find out.

Only the two trees knew the answer.

A MASTERPIECE

Here is a capsule close-up of that strange man Salvador Dali, beginning with a little-known tale of an official art hoax, done by him as an important commission. It isn't often that a great collector gives the stamp of approval to a copy of a great painting, nor that he has the wit and panache to do so openly. But everything happens to Salvador Dali, including the experience of creating an official hoax.

This story concerns the copy he made of a painting by Vermeer, the great Dutch painter. He did it for 'the Grand Seigneur' of medieval art in the USA, the late American banker, Robert Lehman, who discussed the episode with me just after the painting was finished.

Dali's temperature always rises at the mention of Vermeer and has done so ever since he was a boy. His feverish idolatry for his chosen god took an unexpected turn when Robert Lehman (whose world-famous Renaissance collection was recently willed to New York City's Metropolitan Museum of Art) commissioned him: 'Make me a Vermeer!'

Mr Lehman originally got to know Dali in 1934 when the surrealist first arrived in the USA. A mutual friend introduced them, knowing both had a passion for realism and for the paintings of the Middle Ages. Dali was overwhelmed by the Lehman collection. 'But your collection's incomplete, Monsieur. You haven't got a Vermeer!'

'You are right. One has never been put on the market,' Mr Lehman admitted. 'I have searched the world for a Vermeer. I know that one is badly needed to round off my collection.'

ON DEMAND

Suddenly he had an impulse. 'Why don't you make a copy of a Vermeer for me, Mr Dali?'

The painter was overcome, too vain not to be flattered. 'It is impossible, Monsieur. Impossible! Even I could not do it!'

The suggestion lay fallow for a very long time. The men met frequently in the following twenty years but it wasn't until the mid–fifties that Lehman repeated his offer. This time Dali took the bait, with a surprising admission.

'I'm just working on Vermeer's 'Lace-Maker' now – one of the most beautiful paintings ever created!'

'I'll buy it if I can see it first,' Lehman said.

'Of course I will show it to you,' exclaimed Dali. 'I will do it at once! But only on one condition: you must pay me as much for this copy as for a Dali original. Ten thousand dollars. I will make you a perfect copy. . .' (At an auction at Christies in March 1981, his 'Le Sommeil' fetched the highest price ever paid for a work by a living artist, £360,000.)

Dali was, in fact, actually working in the Louvre on the copy, faithfully, painstakingly (no doubt, with banker Lehman's earlier suggestion in mind). But he didn't sit down to paint without making the usual Daliesque demands (of the Louvre in Paris, he claimed!). When I asked him to describe those efforts, he listed them this way:

'First analyse Vermeer colours. . .

'Then ask Louvre for analysis of pigments. . .

'After, order some canvas to be woven. . .just like Vermeer's.'

Before starting on the canvas, Dali also claims he asked the Louvre what ten books Vermeer loved best (so he could read them!), to have absorbed everything he could about the Jesuit ritualism of Vermeer's period, to have read every reference book which Vermeer had presumably consulted about perspective. Finally, he examined, with microscopic care, how Vermeer applied his paint.

He tried to discover exactly what size brushes (down to the number of hairs in each) Vermeer must have used in order to paint with his exact precision. He even tried to determine why Vermeer frequently put maps into his paintings. He read the geography of Vermeer's time. Probably no other painter knows more about Vermeer (if all of this is true).

When Dali finally decided that his own painting was a flawless copy of Vermeer's masterpiece, he submitted the work with his usual devastating bravado to Mr Lehman, who promptly bought it. The banker later described the copy to me as 'glorious'. 'Everyone,' he pointed out, 'agrees it is a remarkable example of Dali's craft, a perfect Vermeer!'

Mr Lehman asked Dali why the canvas was so coarse. This baffled Dali, since he had ordered one to be made to the Louvre's detailed specification of Vermeer's original. Theodore Rousseau, one of the directors of the Metropolitan Museum of Art, pointed out that the original Vermeer canvas at the Louvre had been lined and had shrunk flat, and that time had done much to it in the centuries since it was painted.

Dali's reaction was to order that his canvas be relined, pressed, and flattened out until it was conceded by everyone that it was a perfect copy. The 'masterpiece' had been done without hoaxing a single person at any stage of the game.

It is signed, quite simply, 'Vermeer by Dali'.

POT AU

Anyone who knew or read books or stories by the late Ludwig Bemelman must recall him as one of the great story-tellers of his time. In print and in person he could, in his offhand way, with his delightful suspicion of an accent, make even a near tragedy into something very, very funny.

As in so many men of humour, tragedy managed to follow him – in his case, in the form of a killer disease. Before he died, and knowing how soon that would occur, I wrote him in Paris, asking if he wouldn't like me to arrange an exhibition of his highly personal and completely disarming drawings, which I wanted Londoners to see.

He wrote back in the form of a drawing of a coffin, tall candles lit beside it, a hand thrust high out of the coffin, holding an incongruous flower. Above it he wrote: 'I take your advice. Bless you and thank you, but I think I will wait to be shown in London *après ma mort.*'

Most of the time, he liked to tell stories of himself; this one is hilarious to anyone with the imagination to visualize the actual occasion as he described it. He was living in Paris at the time, but on one visit to London, he regaled us with this and other lunatic tales.

He had been driving rather amiably, in no rush at all, musing about life – destination Paris, on a major road on a long flat plain. On his right was the smaller disused road the new one had replaced, generally totally devoid of traffic.

On this particular day, a motorcyclist drove along the old road at much his same moderate pace, going parallel and at

CHOCOLAT

similar speed in the same direction. The two roads gradually grew closer and closer together until they joined – and the inevitable happened. They collided.

The motorcycle, being lighter than Bemelman's car, flew into the air on impact; the body on it, being lighter still, flew further. Bemelman, white, with a degree both of concern and rage, stopped and leapt from his car, walking toward what must surely be a corpse.

He was somewhat surprised when the presumed corpse got up, shook himself clean of dust and said solemnly: 'Sorry, Sir.' It was his butler.

One could write a whole new book of stories by bringing to mind the ones which were told by Bemelman to his friends. He once told the unlikely but true account of the caste system in a swank Paris restaurant frequented by the rich and expense-society clientele – which led to a broken marriage.

He neatly encapsulated the secret world of the men who served food there – describing in minute detail the ladder every member of the staff had to climb before ending up at the top of it as *Maître d'Hôtel*. This description was, in fact, merely a prelude before he nose-dived into the story, worthy of Feydeau, about one of the restaurant's regular diners.

After the climb from kitchen to bus boy (or 'commis') to waiter, head waiter, then (with immense luck and years of waiting) one became master of all he surveyed – the *Maître* himself. Each level of each career had its own perks, whether in money or food. The next-to-the-top position belonged to waiters who commanded enough respect and friendship from the *Maître* to be given a regular patron to serve – someone whose habits were so fixed one could make some profit out of them.

This story focused on one particular waiter who had a very special daily patron for lunch (a man whom I, too, knew). The waiter soon got to know all about him (either by eavesdropping or by watching); he was a Paris commissionaire who always brought a customer (usually an American) to whom he busily tried to sell something. Always immersed in his deal, he never once looked at his bill: he simply signed it with immense panache before handing it back to the waiter.

This was a very splendid situation for the waiter. One of his favourite items on the daily menu was the rich dark *pot au chocolat*, which was a notable speciality of the restaurant. He simply ordered one for himself every lunch time, putting it on the commissionaire's bill.

The story took an unexpected turn when the man married his office bookkeeper. Bored by a sudden life of idleness, the newly-wealthy woman demanded and got the job of paying the bills, which she did with skill and despatch, scrutinizing

CHOCOLAT

every item, checking and double-checking every amount. When it came to her husband's restaurant chits, she eventually grew concerned. *Pot au chocolat* every day? She knew her husband hated chocolate, so who was he secretly taking to lunch who ordered it regularly?

Suspicion and jealousy gradually took over. She began to surmise all sorts of situations until finally she hired a detective to see what her husband was up to.

The detective's first port of call was, of course, the restaurant, and the first to be questioned was the waiter. 'What woman is he bringing here regularly? We know *he* doesn't eat chocolate, so *she* must be ordering it. Describe her to me!'

The waiter, aware of coming disaster and very fond of his patron, insisted vociferously that he seldom (if ever) had a female guest. He could do this with sincerity.

Obviously not willing to collaborate with evidence, the detective gave up the waiter to take off in other directions. He trailed the man daily and, to his delight, captured his quarry.

The commissionaire did have a mistress. His wife sued him for divorce.

MRS RABINOWITZ

Easter in New York was a ritual in the days when couturier Valentina and her late husband, George Schlee, celebrated it in their sumptuous East River apartment. Being Russian, Valentina supplied all the expected ingredients – mainly the delicious and genuine Russian food which testified to her origin. To this were added large supplies of glamour – and hours of story-telling.

Their guests always included a large dollop of New York's funniest raconteurs; tears often fell as all listened to their stories. Somehow, on one such occasion, I was coaxed into participating; this I did by telling a story about a Russian rabbi, which seemed to me to be patently appropriate.

The religious gentleman of the story had neither temple nor fixed abode. He lived on the road, an itinerant rabbi who went over long reaches of Russia by horse and wagon, travelling with a ragged driver, moving from town to town at a slow pace over bad roads.

The area was so large he was unlikely to reach any village or hamlet more frequently than twice a year. His arrival was always marked by cries of welcome. The village women plied him with gifts made in anticipation – woollen mittens, caps and scarves. Food was never a problem because much of this, too, was cooked and baked for him to take away.

Once in a village, he'd climb down from the wagon and walk to the centre of the village square to be slowly encircled by his congregation, a popular visitor who brought religion to faraway places.

GOES WEST

It mattered not what he preached or even who he was. There was always the pent-up yearning to worship. Nor did it matter that he gave the same sermon from town to town, from year to year. No one remembered.

On one such trip, after leaving a village, his driver suddenly exploded in anger. He'd driven the horse for years, he'd stayed out of sight, he saw the gifts being given. Turning to the rabbi, he burst out in protest: 'You always give the same sermon. You always get the gifts. I've heard you so often I know every word by heart. I could give it myself. It's not fair!' he cried out.

The rabbi listened calmly and quietly and reasonably. He finally came to a conclusion: 'You are right. It is not fair. In the next village, you may give the sermon and I will be your driver. You will get the gifts and the food and you will feel the warmth of their welcome.'

He kept his promise, changing clothes and seats before the next port of call. Just as he promised, the driver delivered the sermon with skill, word for word, emphasizing the right places. As expected, he received all the gifts. He was deliriously happy, finding it hard to conceal it.

But this time, there was one terrible difference. Someone in the crowd (for the first time ever) held up his hand and asked a rabbinical question, obscure and difficult to answer – leaving the man stunned, tongue-tied and deflated. Helpless, he was ready to reveal the truth when a flash of genius came to his rescue.

Turning to the congregation with sudden élan he replied, with shattering contempt:

'Such a stupid question deserves a stupid answer. I'll ask my driver!'

My story was an instant success. Amid the laughter, I suddenly felt a rap on my shoulder from someone behind. 'Don't you know where you are? Don't you know what you've just done? You have told a 'Rabinowitz' story and you are hereby tapped for membership in the Rabinowitz Society!'

Thus I became a member of one of the most exclusive clubs in New York, limited in number to a dozen or more, including such names as John Gunther, George Schlee, Valentina and Garbo.

The Society met infrequently but when they did the purpose was to contribute Rabinowitz-like stories to add to the mythology of a non-existent man.

The fake Mr Rabinowitz steadily evolved as a real person. Every story, every joke, every anecdote that could be attributed to him had its name changed – and was added to the collection which began in the forties when a notable figure in the world of American advertising, Albert Lasker, invented the idea of the Rabinowitz Society.

Rabinowitz soon began to breathe and live. He became the man who always came out on top, whatever the situation. He got into endless difficulties, he married several times (always disastrously), had stupid children, everything possible happened to him. Story after story, joke after joke, added to the characterization. My Russian story was instantly converted. The driver was, of course, the young Rabinowitz before he emigrated to America. 'Even in his young days, he was getting the best of an awkward situation!'

Mr Rabinowitz was soon so perfectly realized, so recognizable, so real, that the late noted playwright member of the Club, S. N. Behrman, seriously intended to write his biography.

Not all stories were about Rabinowitz himself. Members contributed stories to add to those about his mythical family – always in trouble, always a nuisance and always a trial for the long-suffering man. Everyone felt sorry for poor Mr Rabinowitz even though he always won in the end.

GOES WEST

One supposedly true story was quickly added to the mythical biographical data – about a trip made by the fairly stupid wife of a tailor who actually worked in the garment district of New York's Seventh Avenue. His wife was a woman whose talkativeness nearly drove the tailor mad. Whenever she got too much for him, she was shunted off to visit a relative. Once, when he was at his wits' end, he saved enough money to ship her off to her sister working in Los Angeles' garment-making district.

Knowing her proclivity for getting everything wrong, he took time off from work to take her to the airport – right out to the gate, carefully pointing out which of the two planes standing together was the one she must board. This was in the days when boarding a plane could be a hazardous guess. His final command was made for the sake of other passengers on the flight; he loudly announced, 'Remember, you are not to say one word to anyone on the plane. Be quiet and don't talk!'

As expected, she boarded the wrong plane, and had to be taken off and rushed in the nick of time to the one destined for Los Angeles. Breathless and worried, she fell into the first vacant seat she saw – on the aisle, next to a man with head buried in his work.

Getting her breath back, she slowly surveyed the situation. She was obviously sitting next to a diplomat, she decided. She knew it because his hair was greying at the temples, he was reading official-looking papers and he looked terribly important.

She knew she must not disturb him – and she didn't, for at least an hour. But it eventually got to be too much for her to stay silent. Choked with a longing to talk, she turned to the man beside her. Poking him in the ribs with her elbow, she looked at him with a broad smile and asked, 'Are you Jewish?'

'No, Madam, I am not,' the gentleman responded, politely but firmly, then promptly turned back to his documents.

An hour later, she couldn't bear the silence any longer. Poking him in the ribs again, she demanded, 'Not even on your mother's side?'

'No, Madam, I'm not,' he coldly but politely repeated.

Another hour later, she insisted, 'Not even on your father's side?'

Amused as much as annoyed by her persistence and wishing to cut the game short, he looked her straight in the face and said, 'Yes. I am.'

'What!' she exclaimed – almost with a scream. '*You'd never know it!*'

GOES WEST

The story was too good to overlook when told at a Rabinowitz Society meeting. She immediately became Mr Rabinowitz's third wife; a true story became fiction in the saga of little Mr Rabinowitz's life.

A DEBT

The late Camille Bombois was a naïf painter who may one day be considered another Rousseau. He was born in poverty and died in similar circumstances, though quite needlessly. As with Georges Braque, Simone Gauthier of Paris and I used to call on him regularly.

The elderly man and his wife lived in a poor quarter of Paris, in a tiny, sparsely furnished and very ugly little house. Bitterness prevented Bombois from enjoying greater comfort and recognition before he died; he often went so far as to refuse to give his work to dealers whom he thoroughly distrusted. His suspicions almost isolated him. He preferred not to sell at all rather than be, as he thought, 'exploited' by the entrepreneurs. But in a locked closet in the house were many of the finest fruits of his labour – a treasure-trove which, if sold, would not only have provided wider acclaim, but many luxuries denied to the lonely pair.

He had endured a lifetime of hardship which began with the years he served as a labourer in a circus (the background to his early paintings of clowns), so he clung tenaciously to most of his canvases as an insurance for his old age.

Hard as his grip was on these paintings, his wife's was firmer, quite understandably. Her husband was very old; he had suffered several near-fatal illnesses. If death came, his widow would feel safer with a long, narrow, crowded cupboard. Here, indeed, was plentiful insurance.

Actually she died in 1964, before Bombois, of heart failure, leaving him lonelier and more bitter. He had lost most

REPAID

of his sight through carbon monoxide poisoning from his boiler.

Each time Simone and I came to see the old man and his wife, which was about twice a year, we always brought along a pâté de foie gras or some other delicacy. It would invariably be rushed out of sight to some secret hiding-place to be relished after we'd gone. We'd sit in a fairly empty parlour, discussing his work and his bitterness towards dealers, which I tried to placate in his own interest. Slowly, over the years, a feeling of trust developed.

I, at least, was able to buy some of his paintings at the current market price. Among these paintings are several I commissioned, including one of lions: there are also three which I actually roughly sketched out for him to interpret in his own style. I particularly love one which is a stiff parade of earthenware flowerpots, each planted with a different stiff solitary bloom (my ten favourite flowers).

One spring day, Simone and I arrived to find the man close to tears, obviously frightened into a state of near-hysteria. What had happened? we anxiously enquired. Apparently the French income-tax authorities had just discovered his existence. What could he do? He'd end up in jail, he moaned, wringing his hands. His white-faced wife was even more certain of it.

As this was in the early fifties, before French income-taxes were taken too seriously, we finally persuaded them that the tradition for French painters to ignore taxes was an accepted fact. That he wouldn't end up in jail. That no other painter had. And that I would arrange for *Look* magazine's French attorney to look after M. Bombois.

This was done. The case was resolved as all other income-tax matters concerning French painters seemed to be, at least in those days. I never asked what had been done: I was told by the Maître to 'forget it, it was working'.

About five months later, I was back in Paris and went out to see the old couple. This time we were greeted by warm faces wreathed in smiles. A round table was quickly drawn into the centre of the terrible little parlour which smelt of ersatz lino-leum. Upright chairs were drawn to the table for four to sit around. This was something new; obviously a conference was in mind.

After a few moments both M. and Mme Bombois got to the point: How could they possibly thank me for what I'd done? For months, the painter explained, they both worried and fretted about 'how to repay the generous American lady who saved me from jail'. No matter how I insisted he would never have been imprisoned, the fact wouldn't register. They had come to a decision. I simply had to be repaid.

Oh Lord! They're going to offer me a painting, I quickly thought. . .I couldn't possibly accept it. . .I mustn't accept it. . .They had the whole thing out of proportion. . .I must discipline myself not to take anything – not to let them over-estimate what needed to be done.

'Madame Cowles, we have thought it over, my wife and I, and we have at last found the solution,' Bombois firmly announced.

'Please! There is no need for one,' I insisted.

'We've made up our minds. You know that painting that you have always wanted – the one which I've always refused to sell to you?'

'Yes, of course,' I admitted.

'Well, we have finally decided that you can buy it. The price is high because we don't really want to sell it!'

FLOWERS FOR

Madrid, being the capital of a formal Catholic society, was in deep mourning, highly shocked by the sudden death of the beloved wife of a Spanish Cabinet Minister. Apart from her official position, the dead woman had enjoyed an enormous circle of friends, and was highly popular in her own right.

The news came to a woman friend of mine who was in Paris with her husband, an Ambassador to Spain from a small Central American government. He had gone on government business; she had something else on her mind. The couple had five teenage children and no money of their own. They had to use the greatest possible financial skill to keep up a diplomatic front in affluent Madrid. Even going to Paris with her husband meant a difficult expenditure.

The cable announcing the Minister's wife's death was a blow for many reasons. First of all, it meant cutting short their rare Paris trip; secondly, it gave no time to the wife to prowl through the shops on her secret errand. For months she had 'stolen' small amounts from her household money to keep for Paris, where it was her dream to buy her first really extravagant hat.

The trip occurred during the time when women wore floral pieces created to look like crowded gardens on their heads. The Ambassadress knew that such a splendid creation would do her very well for a very long time and, in particular, would give a stylish look to her ubiquitous inexpensive little black dress.

A FUNERAL

The cable suggesting that they return didn't deter her; while her husband hustled through business in order to take an early plane to Madrid, she rushed off to buy the hat, which would have to be selected quickly from one couture millinery collection. She fled to the address of the one she thought would be the most exciting.

Her secret fund was barely enough to pay for the hat she chose but, with a heavy sense of guilt, she tossed discretion to the air. When she boarded the plane she clutched a box with the expensive concoction inside, having persuaded the milliner to let her take the original model.

Once in Madrid, her immediate duty was to pay a call on the family of the dead woman. From other experiences, she knew the form: the woman's mother would be receiving guests in their great salon and everyone in politics, diplomacy and society would be filing through the door.

She wanted to look her best so the precious new hat came out of the box to wear. When she got to the dead woman's house, her spirits suddenly fell. It was a childish notion, she realized, to come in such a gloriously coloured bonnet. Greatly embarrassed, she removed it before ringing the doorbell; when let in, she carefully placed the beautiful object on a bench in the entrance hall.

For an hour or so she sat with all the mourners. She was not the only hatless one and, as she was in black, she felt properly attired. Finally a move was made by all the guests to go. They were then invited to pass by the coffin so each solemnly filed into the next room, which was a bower of flowers. The coffin itself was blanketed in blooms, like one massive bouquet.

She nearly fainted as she neared the body. There, capping a huge mountain of roses and lilies, was a tight brilliant bouquet

A FUNERAL

— *her hat*! A very stupid maid had interpreted the 'bundle' on the bench as her floral offering. It was quietly placed on the coffin with all the other bouquets!

She never saw it again.

THE PEARL

Two sisters living near New York were involved in this story, told me many years ago by their greatest friend:

The two sisters were lively and irresponsible. They grew up in a huge and remarkable home with two remarkable parents, one a saint, the other an eccentric. As long as they could remember, the atmosphere and the rhythm of life in the mansion they called home was charged with financial confusion; family fortunes regularly tobogganned from riches one year, to poverty the next – in fact, they were very very rich on the one hand and on the other too penniless for ordinary necessities.

Father was soft-hearted and untalented, the son who inherited his family's vast fortune and spent the rest of his life losing it. He never really did anything. Work for him consisted of wandering in from time to time to his broker's office (with devastating consequences), to buy and sell the securities which provided their only income.

Few men have been born with less money-sense: he bought and sold on some secret impulsive system which could on occasion cost the family a year's hard living. Other times, if things went well, father's splurge pushed his family immediately back into a life of wild and happy extravagance.

Mother provided the strength. She weathered the shifts from riches to embarrassingly empty purses without fuss or complaint, even nodding with calm approval whenever father made his visits to the pawnbroker.

Everything was done with a view to keeping face with the

NECKLACE

world outside. The house (twice too big for even the plum years) had to be kept up and lived in: all appearances of wealth had to be maintained, at any price.

The *price* was the pawnbroker. Valuable chairs, paintings, family silver and jewellery went back and forth to be pawned in a remote down-town Manhattan stand-by whenever money was short. The pawnbroker knew all the family secrets but he was safely out of their circle, and silent. Most things were eventually ransomed from his shop when money was available, and returned to the rambling Long Island mansion. Some of the regular pawnable valuables spun back and forth like a shuttle over the years.

Mother's one and only passion was her triple string of magnificent real pearls, which she contrived at all costs to keep from father's acquisitive fingers. The fashion for cultivated pearls had not yet occurred; there was a huge financial value as well as a sentimental value to the necklace and mother lived in constant terror that it, too, might end up at the pawnbrokers. To avoid the uncertainty, she finally collected, with consummate skill, an identical, but fake, three-strand necklace – a remarkably fair copy, in fact, of her own pearls.

These were casually allowed to lie loose on her dresser-top or coiled inside a box with her other jewellery. The real necklace was always hidden in the flour crock, inside the coffee tins, rolled up with her stockings or in altogether odd places which changed regularly. Although she completely fooled father, the girls knew where they were hidden.

The game was probably unnecessary; father obviously understood they were untouchable. No matter how bad the money situation was he never even mentioned pearls.

A terrible drama occurred when mother – that seemingly healthy, strong bulwark of the family – had a heart attack in her sleep and was found dead in the morning. Not one member of the family either knew or suspected she was ailing.

The handsome woman was prepared for burial with tender care and pride by her doting family. The fine pearls, which she cherished all her life, glistened on her throat – a monument to a life-long battle to retain them.

The night before she was buried, a thought began to nag at the elder daughter: about those pearls; hadn't mother clung to them with more than personal vanity? Wasn't she protecting them to pass on as a legacy? In her bed as she lay awake, troubled and nervous, the girl pondered the wisdom of burying mother with them.

Finally, controlling her fear and revulsion, she tiptoed downstairs to the parlour where the body lay. Pale with anguish, with shaking fingers, she removed the handsome necklace of real pearls and replaced them with the fakes which she'd filched from the back of mother's dresser-drawer. Ill, almost hysterical, she returned to her bed and spent a grim, sleepless night. No one ever guessed what had been done in the quiet of the night.

But as days went by, she kept losing her nerve and postponing the moment when she knew she had to tell her father and sister what she had done. Months later, neurotic and distressed, she found herself hysterically telling it all during a family discussion about the future of the big house.

'I have something awful to tell you,' she announced. 'It is a horrible secret I have been keeping from you since mother was buried. It is about her pearls!

'I knew she didn't mean to have her necklace buried with her. I'm sure she'd have asked us not to do this if she had known she was dying.

'I simply could not get off my mind how much trouble she'd taken all her life to protect them. . .or about the fake pearls which were supposed to keep you from pawning them, father. . .or how she was constantly thinking up new places to hide the real ones – I suddenly realized it was my obligation, as the eldest daughter, to go on nursing them. . .

'I did a terrible thing. I slipped downstairs the night before she was buried, and exchanged the real ones for the copies I knew were in her drawer.'

As she told her story her sister looked ill. Her face turned almost green with horror.

'*What time did you do that?*' she managed to whisper.

'Just a few minutes after one o'clock,' the older sister explained. 'I remember how frightened I was when the clock banged out one loud note as I opened the door to the parlour.'

'Oh, my God!' her young sister sobbed. 'I had the same thought – the same idea. I sneaked down myself to exchange the pearls. But it was three o'clock in the morning when I did it. . .'